MEXICO IN YOUR POCKET

MEXICO IN YOUR POCKET

A STEP-BY-STEP GUIDE
AND TRAVEL ITINERARY

**BY STEVE ROGERS
AND TINA ROSA**

PREFACE BY CARL FRANZ

Horizon Books

British Library Cataloguing in Publication Data
Rogers, Steve
Mexico in your pocket: a step-by-step guide and travel itinerary.—(Pocket travellers).
1. Mexico—Visitors—Guides
I. Title II. Rosa, Tina III. Series
917.2'04834
ISBN 1-85461-045-7

For Maki and Muriel

Maps Jim Wood
Cover Map Tim Clark

This edition first published in 1990 by Horizon Books Ltd, Plymbridge House, Estover Road, Plymouth PL6 7PZ, United Kingdom. Tel: Plymouth (0752) 705251. Telex: 45635. Fax: (0752) 777603.

Typeset by Kestrel Data, Exeter
Printed in Great Britain by BPCC Wheatons Ltd, Exeter

CONTENTS

Preface 6
How to Use This Book 8
Itinerary 17
Arrival in Mexico City 21
Tour 1 Explore Mexico City 28
Tour 2 Mexico City and Teotihuacán 31
Tour 3 Mexico City—San Miguel 38
Tour 4 San Miguel de Allende 44
Tour 5 San Miguel—Guanajuato 47
Tour 6 Guanajuato—Pátzcuaro 54
Tour 7 Pátzcuaro—Janitzio—Mexico City 58
Tour 8 Mexico City—Oaxaca 60
Tour 9 Tlacolula and Ruins 66
Tour 10 Monte Albán 68
Tour 11 Oaxaca—San Cristóbal 73
Tour 12 San Cristóbal de las Casas 76
Tour 13 San Cristóbal—Palenque 79
Tour 14 Palenque 81
Tour 15 Palenque—Mérida 86
Tour 16 Mérida 90
Tour 17 Mérida—Chichén Itzá—Isla Mujeres 93
Tour 18 Isla Mujeres 99
Tour 19 Isla Mujeres 101
Tour 20 Isla Mujeres—Cobá 102
Tour 21 Cobá—Return to Mérida 105
Post-Tour Options
Mexico City 107
Taxco 108
Pacific Beaches 108
Practical Extras
Culture Shock 111
Speaking Spanish 111
Mexican Food 117
Crafts and Folk Art 123
Fiestas 125

PREFACE

Reading *Mexico in Your Pocket* brought back a rush of memories from my first trip in 1964, when Steve tempted me out of college with an offer I couldn't refuse: a tour of a distant country called Mexico. It was an eye-opening and unforgettable experience, a non-stop series of exotic sights and adventures that would eventually lead me to a career as a travel writer.

Throughout that trip—which roughly followed this book's itinerary—Steve treated me to his famous 'Mexico monologue', an impassioned, off-the-cuff travelogue punctuated by 'Look at that!', 'Did you see that?' and 'I'll bet you didn't know that . . .' His interest in Mexico was all-consuming and highly contagious. No detail was allowed to escape my attention, and I can still feel Steve's elbow in my ribs as he gleefully pointed out yet another stunning view, quaint burro or picturesque colonial ruin. Meals became rest stops, with Steve eagerly poring over the menu as if it were a treasure map, urging me to sample the *cochinita pibil* rather than the more familiar chicken tacos, the *huachinango* rather than the club sandwich. Our curiosity about Mexico, and the hospitality of the people we met along the way, gradually drew us deeper and deeper into the country. It wasn't long before our road map was thumbed beyond repair and our guidebooks were exhausted. A trip that began as a lark was now an odyssey. We travelled from the ordinary to the unexpected, from the unusual to the outrageous. 'This is it!' Steve cried. 'This is the real Mexico!'

As I learned on my first trip, Mexico is a huge and diverse country. Its distinct foreignness, however, can be an obstacle as well as an attraction, even for the experienced traveller. No wonder, then, that so many people throw their hands into the air when the time comes to decide: How, when and where do we begin? With Puerto Vallarta or Coatzacoalcos? Shall we explore the ruined cities of Cobá and Chichén Itzá or laze on the beaches of Oaxaca? Does anyone know when the train leaves for Lake Pátzcuaro?

Mexico in Your Pocket has the answers, along with a figurative elbow in the ribs, as Steve and Tina share both their enthusiasm for Mexico and comprehensive, up-to-date advice on everything from their favourite hotels to shopping tips for Indian textiles. Travellers will find a detailed, do-it-yourself itinerary combined with the kind of personal advice and 'Look at that!' encouragement that makes this a genuine guide rather than just another directory of well-known sights.

Steve and Tina's suggested itinerary covers Mexico from Baja to the Yucatán, with never a dull moment in between. If you find yourself exhausted by the pace, slow down. When you discover a place you can't bear to leave, don't. For many people, the true pleasures of travel are found in getting to know a few places well, rather than globetrotting from A to Z. Whatever your preference, *Mexico in Your Pocket* is easily adapted to your own budget and style of travel. Use the book as a start-to-finish travel plan or take it area by area, as an excellent list of Mexico's classic and yet-to-be-discovered sights.

Explore Mexico for yourself and you'll discover, as so many of us have, that the excitement never ends.

Carl Franz

When Tina first went to Mexico from New York she was planning on a two-week holiday. It took her 8 years to get back to New York. If this is your first trip to Mexico, be warned! It may be the beginning of a long love affair.

HOW TO USE THIS BOOK

This book is your pocket-sized 'tour guide'. It provides you with the travel efficiency of an organised tour along with the freedom and flexibility that independent travellers enjoy.

Mexico in Your Pocket presents a tried and proven itinerary for sampling the best that Mexico has to offer—ancient ruins, Indian market-places, colonial history, tropical beaches and lots more—with maximum value for money.

Like every good itinerary, it also allows for change according to your personal interests and whims. Customise this itinerary and make it your own. Make changes. Take a pencil and draw lines through some sentences, circles around others; scribble notes in the margins. As you talk to other travellers, refine your plan further. Spend more time in the places that intrigue you and skip those that don't. If a place bores you, leave early, substitute a side trip or schedule an extra day on the beach.

In this itinerary you'll find:

1. An **Introductory Overview** for each tour.
2. An hour-by-hour **Suggested Schedule** for each tour.
3. A list of **Sightseeing Highlights** (rated: ●●● Don't miss; ●● Try hard to see; ● Worthwhile if you can make it).
4. **Transport** tips and instructions, including self-guided walking tours of sightseeing highlights.
5. **Food** and **Accommodation**: How and where to find the best places in your price range, including addresses, phone numbers and our favourites.
6. **Orientation** and an easy-to-read **Map** of the area.
7. **Helpful Hints** on shopping and other incidents of Mexican travel.
8. **In-Tour Extensions** for those who have more time. Suggestions for exploring the area in more depth.

At the end of the book you'll find chapters presenting **practical information** and **cultural insights** to enhance your trip.

How much will this trip cost?

Mexico's inflation rate is astounding to many foreigners. So is the declining value of the peso, which translates into *increasing* value of other currencies. All this economic see-sawing makes travel costs in Mexico unpredictable, but we'll stick our necks out and hazard some rough 'guestimates'.

These price estimates are based on one person's travelling

expenses. The actual 'per person' expense depends on how many people are in your party. Solitary travellers can expect to spend somewhat more. Group expeditions may spend less per person on hotel rooms and taxi fares; costs per person of restaurant meals and most public transport will be the same no matter how many people are travelling together. Excluding costs of air fares to and from Mexico, peso-pinching 'budget' travellers can do this trip for about £450 (about £21 a day) per person. They'll take buses wherever possible and never hire a car or a taxi for day trips.

'Moderate' travellers should budget about twice that amount. £850 (£39 a day) per person, based on hiring a car for the Caribbean Loop and hiring taxis for several day trips. The 'De-luxe' traveller will hire cars for the entire trip and can expect to spend £1,300 (about £58 a day).

Should you rent a car?

No question about it—a car is convenient, and most Westerners are used to having one at their disposal. To hire a car in Mexico you must be over 24 years old, have a major credit card and a valid international driver's license. Expect to pay at least £32 a day plus mileage for a standard-size car. Most airports have several hire firms. Shop around for a special deal.

Driving in Mexico is different from elsewhere. An experienced driver should encounter no major problems, but it's hardly relaxing. Driving in Mexico City is nightmarish —avoid it unless you've successfully tackled traffic in Tokyo or Rome or driven in stock car races. If you rent a car for the Colonial Loop, wait until you're ready to leave Mexico City to do so.

In Mexico, where fewer people own cars, public transport is convenient, inexpensive and relatively comfortable. For sightseeing and getting around cities, it is often cheaper to hire a taxi for a day than to hire a car.

Better yet, public transport brings you into closer contact with the people, and the people are half the fun. Bus riding is 'respectable' in Mexico. If you stick to first- and second-class buses (the difference is that first class has a toilet aboard and stops less often) you won't be riding with pigs and goats. To experience *that* you'll need to take third-class buses. Taking third-class buses is a genuine adventure, but you'll never have to take one on this itinerary unless you want to.

We recommend public transport and taxis for the Colonial Loop and Oaxaca-Chiapas legs of your trip and hiring a car for the Yucatán segment. The Yucatán can be done by bus and local day tours, but due to poorer bus service than in other parts of Mexico, it's easier to drive. There's hardly a curve in the roads, traffic is light, there aren't many cities to drive through and the roads are well marked.

If you'll be driving a car on any part of this trip, be sure to read the information on driving in Mexico on pages 63-92 of *The People's Guide to Mexico* (see **Recommended Reading** below).

Hotels

As our old friend Carl Franz says, 'Hotels are just places where you sleep, bathe and get some privacy'. That you can do in any degree of simplicity or comfort you wish. In each town, we suggest hotels in three categories—de luxe, moderate and budget. (Prices are about the same for a single or a double.)

De luxe rooms will cost between £20–£25 unless otherwise specified. These hotels are not Hiltons or Sheratons (which, where they exist, are more expensive), nor are they the most expensive hotels in town. They do provide amenities and conveniences like in-hotel shops and travel agencies.

Moderate hotels cost £10–£16. The moderately priced rooms we've chosen are quite comfortable and, whenever possible, have a colonial flavour.

Budget hotels, with rates in the £5–£10 range, *are not* 'bottom of the line'. You'll have your own bathroom, and the rooms are clean.

Two important considerations in choosing your hotel room are temperature and noise. That upstairs room may have a view of the plaza, but the dedicated sleeper may prefer a darker and quieter interior room. In the Yucatán you'll want a fan or air conditioning; in the hill towns of the Colonial Loop and San Cristóbal, you may want an upstairs room (more heat from sunlight), or one with a fireplace.

Any hotel, however nice, may have its flaw. Once in Cancún we finally found a hotel that we could afford. We moved into our room and Tina blissfully flopped down on the bed. Her expression was not so blissful seconds later when she checked under the bedding and said, unbelieving, 'This bed isn't a bed, it's just a box spring!'

Steve reported this shortcoming to the management. 'What floor are you on?' the manager asked.

'The ground floor.'

'Oh,' he said casually, 'only the first floor rooms have mattresses.'

We slept on the box spring.

When to go

Mexico has two tourist seasons: winter and summer. Spring and autumn are 'off-season'.

In the tropical lowlands, winter is the dry season and temperatures are generally moderate in most coastal areas. Expect temperatures in the 80s with clear days. In the Yucatán the weather is similar except during *nortes* (wind and rain storms) that may last 3 or 4 days.

Winter in the highlands is also dry. It is generally warm and clear during the daytime. At higher elevations and in the north temperatures can drop below freezing at night. Spring is the hottest time of year in the highlands, and it is windy. Expect hot, windy spring weather in coastal areas as well.

The rainy season starts in May and runs to the end of October in most of Mexico. The highlands are often cool and sunny in the morning with cloudbursts in the afternoon. Coastal areas are hot and humid with frequent rain.

Autumn is the hurricane season in the coastal areas. The highlands will be pleasant and green with lessening rain as winter approaches.

When NOT to go

Mexico City more or less empties twice a year—during the Christmas season and *Semana Santa* (Holy Week, before Easter). If you find yourself on a beach you'll think the entire population of Mexico is there with you. Not only beaches but many smaller inland cities such as San Miguel de Allende and Oaxaca are popular spots for Mexican holiday-makers. To escape *Semana Santa*, we once travelled deep into the remote Lacandón jungle; even there, we were not alone! If you travel during one of these holiday times, you *must* make your airline and hotel reservations well in advance.

We always travel without hotel reservations the rest of the year. With a flexible attitude and a willingness to look around a little we've never found ourselves homeless for the night. Look over the list of *fiestas* in the back of this book while planning your trip. It's great to stumble upon a local *fiesta*, but without reservations there could be 'no room at the inn'.

What to bring

Keep these items available in a day pack or shoulder bag:
Water purification drops. Three brands available in Mexican *farmacias* (chemists) and supermarkets are Ni-bac, Elibac and Microdyn. Follow the instructions on the bottle. See how many *gotas* (drops) to use per *litro* (litre).

Toilet paper. Only toilets in the nicest restaurants have toilet paper; public toilets don't. The trick is always to carry a medium-size roll, instead of a big bulky one or a few shreds. If you can work out how to do this, please let us know!
Pepto Bismo. Some travellers recommend taking a daily single dosage of Pepto Bismo starting a week before the trip and continuing for the duration, thus avoiding all stomach complaints. (Except, perhaps, constipation?) This seems a bit like overkill to us. We recommend bringing a bottle along and using it on an as-needed basis for *turista* (the dreaded Montezuma's Revenge). Pepto Bismo is available in most Mexican *farmacias*.
Earplugs. Mexico is *not* a quiet county. Most Mexicans don't even notice background noise, and often find too much silence *muy triste* (very sad). Earplugs, handy for catching a snooze on a bus or aeroplane, also let you turn down the volume on the typical night-time medley of barking dogs and diesel buses and the early morning chorale of church bells, cockerels and burros.
Small hand compass. It will help you follow maps and directions in this book. If you're driving, a compass will also help you navigate through cities.
Small torch. Great for exploring ruins and finding your way around darkened hotel rooms without waking your travel companion. Many hotels don't provide reading lamps.
Mosquito repellent. Particularly necessary in the Yucatán.
Bandana. You can pick up a colourful cotton scarf at any Mexican market. Handy as a sweat rag or headband when exploring ruins, as a flannel or bandage, and for 1,001 other uses.
Plastic water bottle. Gets you through long bus trips and that hot climb to the top of a pyramid.
Swiss Army knife. For peeling fruit and opening bottles along the road.
Hidden pocket or **money belt**. The best insurance against getting stranded without money in Mexico.

What else to bring

As little as possible! Travel with one medium-sized piece of hand luggage and a day pack. If possible, start your trip with the suitcase half empty to leave room for that irresistible handmade spinning wheel and other folk art you'll collect along the way.

You'll also want to bring comfortable walking shoes. Trainers are fine; 10-pound hiking boots are overkill. Bring a warm sweater or jacket for the Colonial Loop hilltowns, or buy a beautiful wool sweater or poncho during your trip. Take quick-dry clothing that you can wash and dry overnight in your hotel room. Bring an adequate supply of film for your camera, since it's expensive in Mexico.

Recommended reading

History and archaeology:
Many Mexicos, Lesley Byrd Simpson (University of California Press). History of Mexico.
Insurgent Mexico, John Reed (Greenwood Press, London). An American journalist's experiences in the Mexican Revolution.
Incidents of Travel in Central America, Chiapas and Yucatán (2 volumes) and *Incidents of Travel in Yucatán* (2 volumes), John Lloyd Stephens (Dover Publications, New York). Travels and adventures of one of the first archaeological explorers in the area.
People of the Serpent, Edward Thompson. Highly readable account of the experiences of the U.S. Consul to the Yucatán for forty years, starting in 1885.
The Blood of Kings—Dynasty and Ritual in Mayan Art, Linda Schele and Mary Ellen Miller. Written as a catalogue for a show of Mayan art by experts who have broken the code of Mayan inscriptions, this beautifully illustrated book presents a new and radical view of Mayan civilisation.

If you want supplementary guidebooks to any of the ruins on your itinerary, the Museum of Anthropology in Mexico City has the best selection.

Also recommended:
Mexico, Michael D Coe (Thames & Hudson)
Mexico, Past & Present, Peter McGregor Eadie (Batsford)
History of Mexican Archaeology: The Vanished Civilisations of Middle America, Bernal (Thames & Hudson)
Ancient Kingdoms of Mexico, Nigel Davies (Penguin)

Culture and sociology:
Distant Neighbors, Alan Riding. In-depth explanation of Mexico's culture and political system, and the historical relationship between Mexico and the United States.
Five Families, Oscar Lewis. Readable study of the Mexican family structure.

Fiction:
Aztec, Gary Jennings. Historical novel of the Aztec empire before and during the Spanish Conquest; insights into pre-Columbian civilisation with lots of gorey details.

The Power and the Glory, Graham Greene (Bodley Head). Novel of a renegade priest forced underground during the Mexican Revolution.
The Bridge in the Jungle, B. Traven, (Cape). Novel about the condition of Indians in Mexico through the first half of this century. We highly recommend this and any of Traven's other books on Mexico.

Travel guides:
The People's Guide to Mexico, Carl Franz (John Muir Publications, Santa Fe). A must! And take it with you! This is the definitive 'how-to' book of Mexican travel—by foot, car, plane, truck, bus, homemade RV, train, burro, kayak and dugout canoe. Carl Franz shows you how to handle just about every situation you may run into. Co-starring Steve! Available from Horizon Books, Plymbridge House, Estover Road, Plymouth PL6 7PZ, UK.

Also recommended:
The Rough Guide to Mexico (Harrap Columbus)
Mexico City (Fodor's 89)
The Shopper's Guide to Mexico, Steve Rogers and Tina Rosa, (John Muir Publications, available from Horizon Books). We're not just tooting our own horn here! This comprehensive guide to folk art and handcrafts supplements our regional guide to the Colonial Loop, Oaxaca Valley, the Yucatán and Mexico City. Let us help you find what you want at the right price.

Scheduling

To follow this itinerary like clockwork, please **arrive in Mexico City on a Friday** in order to enjoy a Saturday market in Oaxaca.

Mexicans list departure and arrival times using the 24-hour clock. Afternoon or p.m. hours are listed as 1300 to 2400. A 2:00 p.m. bus leaves at 1400 (*catorce horas*).

Nothing in Mexico moves *exactly* on schedule. One of the nicest things about Mexico is that it slows you down. People aren't in a hurry, and everything—from restaurants and bus schedules to public services—reflects that. As our friend Eve says, 'Mexicans don't wait for the bus; they hang out, and when the bus comes along they get on it. In Mexico you learn how to "not wait".'

Most stores or offices, including the post office, are closed from 2 to 4 p.m. or from 3 to 5 p.m. for *comida* (the main meal of the day) and *siesta*. To avoid endless frustration (a symptom of 'schedule-itis'), get used to the big hole in the middle of the Mexican day. Many shops reopen until 7 or 8 p.m., making evening a good time for shopping. Most museums are closed on Mondays. You may discover other local idiosyncrasies (for instance, in Pátzcuaro you can't buy alcohol at weekends). Siesta is a good time to read, work on your travel journal, write postcards—or take a siesta yourself.

Documents

To get a tourist card (visa), you must show proof of citizenship—a passport, certified birth certificate, or notarised affidavit of citizenship. A vaccination certificate is not necessary. Your airline or travel agent can get your tourist card for you in advance, or you can pick one up at the Mexican Embassy. In any case you must get it stamped when you enter Mexico. Hang onto it—you'll be required to hand it in when you leave the country. A 30-day card is all you need for this trip, though you can get three- or six-month tourist cards. Any child under 18 travelling to Mexico alone or with another person must have both parents' written, notarised consent. This means, for example, that a father travelling with his son must have the mother's notarised consent to the trip. The rule is not always enforced, but it may be.

Your travel agent will be able to advise you on the best way of getting to Mexico. The only airline offering scheduled flights from London is Continental Airlines, which has daily flights. The cheapest scheduled fare is about £600 return, which requires you to be away a minimum of two weeks and a maximum of three months.

There are several tour operators offering holidays in Mexico, notably Speedbird, Sunset and Kuoni. They all offer complete packages, however, with accommodation provided, which would not suit the independent traveller. However, some of the packages are cheaper than the scheduled flight, so it might be possible to use them to get to Mexico, and 'do your own thing' more or less when you get there. Check with your travel agent.

Another cheap way of getting there is to use one of the so-called 'bucket shops' which offer extra-special deals. They usually advertise in the classified columns of the national press, and their prices can be considerably cheaper than the scheduled fare. Travelling this way will almost certainly mean changing planes, often in some outlandish place at an ungodly hour, but if you don't mind that, it is not a bad way of flying to Mexico.

Once in Mexico, you should check the airline schedules in advance—they are subject to change.

'FE IN DIOS Y ADELANTE!'
(Faith in God and Onward!)
[*Slogan painted on a Mexican lorry bumper*]

ITINERARY

We have to admit that without time limitations we'd probably spend six months taking this trip. Most of us, unfortunately, don't have that luxury but instead must fit our world travel into all-too-brief holidays. If you only have three weeks (or less), this is an excellent itinerary for exploring a lot of Mexico and seeing where you'd like to spend more time later. For example, if the Chiapas jungle fascinates you, plan to explore the Usumacinta River on your next trip.

Colonial architecture, anthropology museums and Mexican art are fascinating—but so is a leisurely afternoon of people-watching in the town plaza or *tianguis* (market). While we've packed just about every hour of every day with sightseeing suggestions, don't hesitate to skip a few in favour of an unexpected adventure.

The trip is divided into three segments. If your holiday time is limited, consider a one-week trip using the Colonial Loop (Tours 1-7) or the Yucatán segment (Tours 16-21 starting and finishing in Mérida). For a two-week trip, go directly to Oaxaca via Mexico City and use Tours 8 to 21. If you have more time—a month or more—add extra relaxation days to your itinerary and head straight for the Pacific beaches.

Here's an overview of the itinerary.

THE COLONIAL LOOP

Remember: Try to arrive in Mexico City on a Friday. On arrival visit the airport tourist information office, get orientated, find your hotel and enjoy a good dinner.

TOUR 1 Your first day in Mexico will be devoted to exploring the sights of Chapultepec Park. You'll visit the Museum of Anthropology, a splendid introduction to Mexico's culture and history. In the afternoon, tour Chapultepec Castle, once the elegant home of the Emperor Maximilian and his wife Carlota. Then see the Museum of Modern Art, the Rufino Tamayo art museum and/or the zoo. In the evening, if you've still got the energy explore the nightlife in the posh Zona Rosa or Garibaldi Plaza.

TOUR 2 This morning you'll take a walking tour of central Mexico City, including the Zócalo (main plaza), the National Palace's Diego Rivera murals depicting Mexico's history, and

Mexico—Itinerary Route

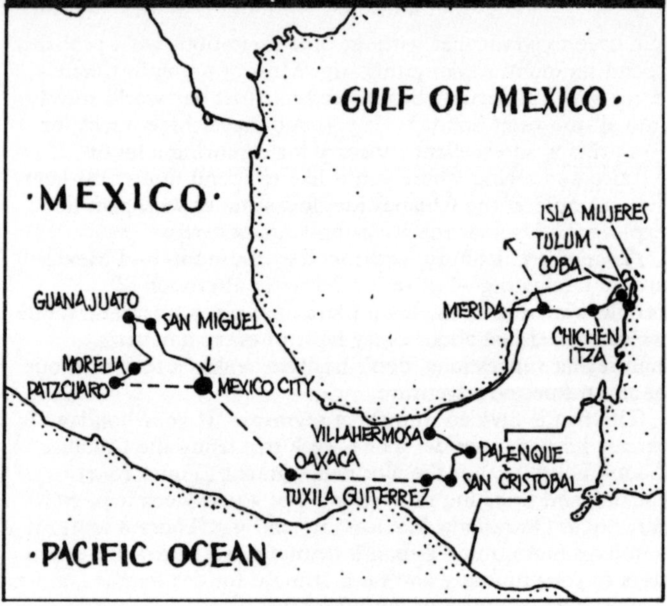

the Templo Mayor, recently discovered Aztec ruins. In the afternoon, tour the pre-Columbian ruins at Teotihuacán. Tonight, perhaps see the Ballet Folklórico.

TOUR 3 Today you'll leave Mexico City by bus or hired car for the colonial hill-town and artist community of San Miguel de Allende. After lunch there will be time for people-watching, window-shopping and a sunset walk.

TOUR 4 Take a morning walk to visit more of the sights of San Miguel. In the afternoon, bus or drive to the sanctuary at Atotonilco, then relax in the hot springs at Las Grutas.

TOUR 5 Leaving San Miguel early, travel to Guanajuato, the beautifully preserved colonial state capital. Enjoy sightseeing around town on foot, and watch the sunset from a scenic viewpoint. After dinner, join in the evening fun on the main plaza.

TOUR 6 Today you'll travel from Guanajuato through Morelia, Michoacán's state capital, to arrive at the Tarascan Indian town of Pátzcuaro. Take a relaxed walk to see the sights.

TOUR 7 After a morning in the Pátzcuaro market, take a boat to the island of Janitzio for lunch. You'll catch an early afternoon bus back to Mexico City.

OAXACA TO PALENQUE

TOUR 8 Arriving in Oaxaca, visit the *tianguis* (Indian market), where you can buy excellent weaving and folk art from colourfully dressed Indians. Take an afternoon walk to see museums and churches. In the evening you may want to watch folk dancers performing at a central hotel.

TOUR 9 Tour the outlying areas of Oaxaca, visiting the Sunday market in Tlacolula and ancient ruins including Mitla and Yagul. On the way back to the city you'll have a chance to visit the village of Teotitlán del Valle and watch some of Mexico's finest weavers at work. After dinner, join the Sunday evening promenade on the plaza with its bandstand and lovely jacaranda trees.

TOUR 10 Exploring the spectacular Zapotec ruins of Monte Albán will be the highlight. You'll also have time for more market-place browsing and shopping.

TOUR 11 A day of hard travelling: travel by bus from Oaxaca to the highland Maya town of San Cristóbal de las Casas, the most Guatemala-like town in Mexico. Check into your hotel and rest.

TOUR 12 Explore San Cristóbal on foot. Later in the afternoon, visit Casa Na-Bolom, the residence and museum of renowned anthropologists Gertrude Duby and the late Frans Blom.

TOUR 13 This morning you'll travel from San Cristóbal to Palenque. After checking into your hotel and making your reservations for Tour 15, you'll have ample time to cool off in the swimming pool and look around town.

TOUR 14 Explore the Mayan ruins of Palenque, a quintessential 'lost city' in the jungle. Spend the rest of the day relaxing in your hotel or exploring the town.

TOUR 15 After experiencing the magnificent waterfalls of Agua Azul, you'll take the bus to Villahermosa to catch your flight to Mérida, your base in the Yucatán.

THE YUCATÁN

TOUR 16 Today is for sightseeing around Mérida, exploring the Museum of Anthropology, visiting the zoo and mingling with Maya Indians in the market-place. In the evening, after feasting on fabulous Mayan cuisine, watch Mérida's Ballet Folklórico.

TOUR 17 Leaving Mérida at dawn's early light, you'll arrive on Isla Mujeres around sunset. On the way, explore the great Maya/Toltec ruins of Chichén Itzá.

TOUR 18 Isla Mujeres is a beautiful tropical island with fine beaches. Enjoy it!

TOUR 19 Go snorkelling at El Garrafón, the beautiful underwater National Park, and see the sea turtles, visiting the Mayan temple at Ixchel for sunset. Or spend another day sunning yourself on the beach.

TOUR 20 Returning by ferry to the mainland, spend a couple of hours at the wildlife sanctuary lagoons of Xel-ha, then visit the magical seaside Mayan ruins at Tulum.

TOUR 21 After investigating Cobá, the least-explored and least-reconstructed ruin on your itinerary, you'll return to Mérida for your last dinner in Mexico and rest for your trip home the next day.

ARRIVAL IN MEXICO CITY

Arrival checklist

■ After claiming your baggage, exchange your money for pesos at the bank in the airport.
■ Go to the Tourist Information booth in Section A of the airport for maps, a hotel reservation if you need one, and information on taxi tickets.
■ Make your Mexico City hotel reservation for Tour 7.
■ Make your airline reservations for Morelia-Mexico City (unless you're hiring a car for the Colonial Loop) and Mexico City-Oaxaca.
■ Buy taxi ticket. Take taxi to your hotel and get settled there.
■ Get your hotel to make reservations for the Ballet Folklórico on Sunday night. (Or you can buy tickets on your walk tomorrow.)
■ Have dinner in your hotel and get a good rest.

Airport orientation

The airport banks are open longer hours than the ones in the city centre and often give a slightly better exchange rate. Most large hotels will accept dollars or traveller's cheques, but usually at a lower exchange rate. You can only exchange money at a bank between the hours of 10:00 a.m. and 1:00 p.m. and it may mean standing in long queues, so we suggest changing enough money to cover your estimated expenses for a week at a time. Try to change enough to get through the following Monday, the busiest day at banks. The Tourist Information Centre will help you make your hotel reservation at no charge. While you're there, get maps of the city and the Metro. Buy a taxi ticket to your hotel, sold at both ends of the terminal. Taxi tickets protect you from being overcharged by voracious cabbies. It's at least a 30-minute trip from the airport to the city centre.

Tourist Information recommends three hotels convenient to the airport, and you'll want to make reservations at one of them for Tour 7 of your itinerary. The **Fiesta Americana** (tel. 762-0199) and the **Holiday Inn** (tel. 762-4088), both on Blvd. Aeropuerto, are expensive by Mexican standards. If you don't want to spend that much, book a room at **El Reazor** (Viaducto Miguel Aleman 297, tel. 657-3062 or 652-4470)—only 7 or 8 minutes from the airport.

Now's the time to buy your airline tickets for later in the itinerary. Book yourself onto Mexican Flight 201 at 6:30 a.m. on Tour 8 from Mexico City to Oaxaca. (Budget travellers may prefer to take 'El Oaxaqueño', the overnight train to Oaxaca. Or take a bus from Terminal de Autobuses de Pasajeros de Oriente next to the metro station San Lazaro on Line 1.)

Mexico City orientation

Welcome to 'The Big Enchilada'!

When Cortés first arrived in Mexico City (then called Tenochtitlán, the Place of the Prickly Pear Cactus) in 1519, it was already larger than any European capital city. It still is. In fact, this awesome megalopolis, whose population is variously estimated at from 18 million to 21 million, is probably the world's largest city. Amazingly, however, the overcrowded populace is usually helpful and friendly. Mexicans call the capital simply 'México' or 'D.F.' (pronounced 'day-effay,' which stands for *distrito federal*).

Mexico City is located 7,500 feet above sea level in a high valley surrounded by mountains. This valley, formally known as the Valley of Anáhuac, was once covered with forests and lakes. The climate is temperate with the temperature hardly ever going below freezing and rarely getting really hot. The rainy season is between the months of May and October, but it occasionally rains at other times as well.

According to legend the Aztecs came to the Valley of Mexico in 1325 and founded the city of Tenochtitlán on an island where they saw an eagle sitting on a nopal cactus with a snake in its beak, as foretold by prophecy. The Aztecs dominated the region and the city grew to an estimated 500,000.

The Spaniards under the leadership of Hernan Cortés arrived in 1519. The Aztecs thought Cortés was the god Quetzalcoátl (the Plumed Serpent—you'll be hearing a lot about him) returning as prophesied. Quetzalcoátl was reputed to be light-skinned with a beard, so Cortés and his men fitted the description. That made it much easier for the small force of around 500 Spaniards, backed up by tens of thousands of Indians who loathed the Aztecs, to besiege the city of Tenochtitlán, capture its leaders and virtually destroy the city in the process. The *conquistadores* enslaved the Indians and started rebuilding the city in European style. They built great cathedrals and palaces with much of the building material coming from the razed Aztec temples and buildings.

The city grew slowly over the years and the lake eventually dried up. By 1930 the population of the city was only one million. Incredible growth has taken place in the last fifty years or so, bringing about the destruction of the valley's

Mexico City Metro

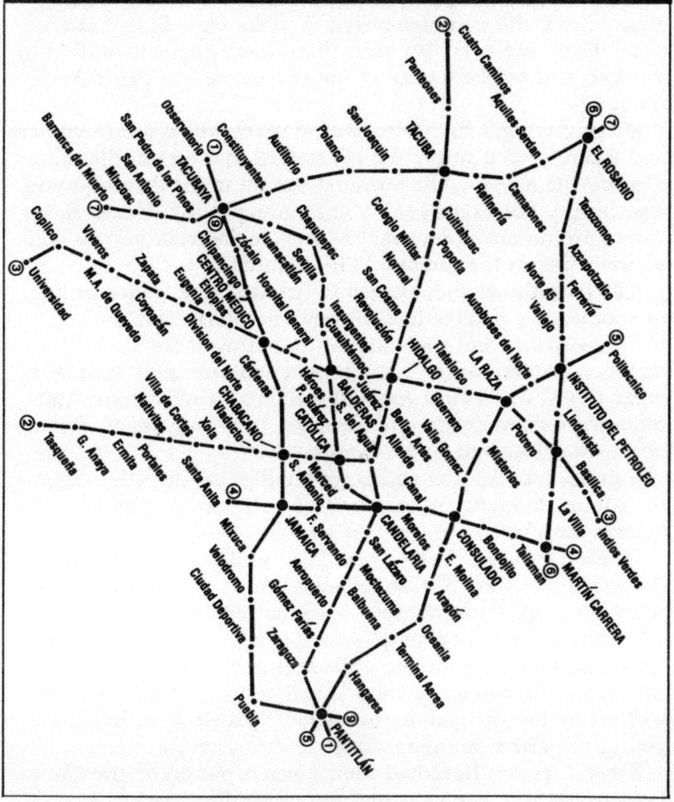

environment as the city's cars, buses and factories spew out a world-class smog. We'll be confining our explorations to only a few areas of this endless urban sprawl: the central historical area, Chapultepec Park and the Zona Rosa, and the pyramids of Teotihuacán, an hour's drive north of the city.

Transport in Mexico City

Mexico City's intricate bus system will get you to any part of the city, however obscure. But you'll find it much simpler to rely on the Metro, *peseros* (shared taxi vans) and taxi cabs.

The Metro: Mexico City's underground has recently had an enormous fare increase! It used to cost one peso to ride;

now it costs 100 pesos to ride anywhere in the city—still the world's best transport bargain. The Metro is surprisingly clean, quick and comprehensive. Tickets are sold five at a time. There are presently nine lines. Each line is identified by a colour and by the names of the two stations at the ends of the line.

Getting around by Metro is easy if you know where you are and where you're going. To get started in the right direction, identify the name of the terminal station in the direction you want to go. For example, if you're going to the Zócalo on Line 2 from your hotel near the Revolución station, you will be travelling in the direction of Tasqueñá.

The map shows the stations for transferring from one line to another. To change lines, follow the signs that say *Correspondencia* and the name of the terminal station in the direction you're going. Some connections are quite simple: at other times, you'll find yourself walking for what seems like miles through underground passages, following arrows up and down escalators and across ramps.

Suitcases, backpacks and large bundles are not allowed on the Metro, though you may be able to get away with it outside rush hours.

Cautionary note: The Grope. Like underground railways the world over, the Big Enchilada's Metro system has its share of creeps with 'the feelies'. Tina carries a large shoulderbag on a long strap, which can be wedged between herself and a likely 'groper'. She also doesn't hesitate to turn and jam a fist into an offender's belly, stamp sharply on his foot or say loudly '*Quítate tus manos!*' ('Keep your hands to yourself!') The timid may prefer to take a cab.

Several friends have had their pockets picked on the Metro. Be sure to carry any valuables in your hidden pocket or money belt. Avoid rush hour Metro travel (7:00-10:00 a.m. and 4:00-7:00 p.m.) at all costs!

Useful Metro vocabulary: *Salida* = Exit. *Andenes* = Boarding platforms.

Peseros: As you might deduce from the name, *peseros* (shared taxis, also called *colectivos* or *combis*) used to charge a single peso for a ride. Nowadays, a ride in a pesero costs about £0.10p, with an additional charge for longer distances. A network of these green and white minibuses covers the entire city. To flag one down, step off the curb into the life-threatening traffic and wave.

Accommodation

For a de-luxe city-centre choice, we recommend the **Hotel**

Majestic (Madero 73, tel. 521-8600). Its handsome tiled lobby with fountain is inviting, and the fifth floor rooms with small balconies offer the best view of the Zócalo.

Our favourite moderately-priced hotel in all of Mexico City is just a ten-minute walk from the Zócalo, right on Plaza Garibaldi, the heart of mariachi music in Mexico. The **Hotel Galícia** (Honduras 11, tel. 529-7791) has attractive and comfortable rooms with colour TV, a perfect retreat from the authentic Mexican musical madness on the plaza. Ask for a quiet room. Our favourite budget-moderate hotel near the Zócalo is the **Hotel Monte Carlo** at Uruguay 69. (A fringe benefit is the location, right around the corner from the Pasteleria Madrid at 5 de Febrero 25, about which one fellow traveller exclaimed, 'I've been planning my vacations around this bakery for 20 years!')

The Zona Rosa, on the south side of Paseo de la Reforma near the Monument to Independence ('the Angel'), is a popular international tourist area noted for exclusive and fashionable shops, restaurants and clubs. Inexpensive lodgings are just about impossible to come by in this area. The charming **Hotel María Christina** at Río Lerma 31 (tel. 546-9880) is your best bet for accommodation at a moderate rate. We also recommend the **Del Angel** at Río Lerma 154 (tel. 533-1032).

For an oxygen-rich atmosphere of greenery and quiet, try the **Hotel Polanco** (Edgar Allen Poe 8, tel. 520-6040) near Chapultepec Park. To avoid noise, be sure to ask for a room '*que no está cerca de la bomba*' ('which isn't near the pump'). The Polanco is right next door to the Restaurant Parador de Manolo, specialising in truly excellent Spanish cuisine.

Which brings us to Steve's favourite subject . . .

Food

You could spend your whole holiday sampling the international cuisine of Mexico City. Thousands of restaurants range from quick-and-simple *loncherías* to those offering full gourmet dinners. Much as Steve would like to, we haven't been able to sample them all; but after prolonged eating, here are some of our favourites. All are moderate to inexpensive. When in the Zócalo area, have lunch at **Fonda Las Casuelas**, República de Colombia 69. Don't let the run-down neighbourhood scare you off. This beautifully-decorated restaurant serves excellent Mexican specialities. Try the *tortilla* soup for a real treat.

The **Hosteria de Santo Domingo** (Belisario Dominguez 72, just off República de Chile) is reputed to be the oldest restaurant in the city. They serve traditional Mexican food, the service is great and the prices are the most reasonable anywhere for a restaurant of this class. If you are in luck, there may be two old gentlemen playing Scott Joplin on piano and violin. Feeling adventurous? Try the *chiles en nogada*, a *chile relleno* variation stuffed with meat and walnuts in a creamy sauce decorated with pomegranate. Another old-fashioned central restaurant is the **Café Tacuba** (Tacuba 28). The typical Mexican food is unexceptional, but it's worth a visit for the atmosphere. You might also try the Sunday lunch buffet at the Hotel Majestic for a great view of the Zócalo and lots of food *estilo ranchero* (country style). Enjoy mariachi music while you eat.

El Danúbio (Uruguay 3) is a very good seafood restaurant with a huge afternoon *comida corrida*. Steve has been making pilgrimages there since 1959, and the *huachinango veracruzano* (red snapper in tomato sauce) has remained excellent. The price, 10 pesos then, has changed, but the waiters are the same, only older. A taxi driver guided us to a less expensive seafood place, **Los Jarochos** (Calle Honduras 17-1, just down from Plaza Garibaldi). The *sopa marinera* (sailor's soup) is excellent but not for the fainthearted as it contains octopus, sardines and all manner of other sea life; served only on weekends.

The huge 'eating market' right off Plaza Garibaldi contains many *fondas*—small market-stall restaurants serving dishes such as *birria* (pit barbecued goat in a juicy sauce), *pozole* (pork and hominy soup) and *carnitas* (delicious pork served with *tortillas* and *salsa*). Competition is fierce and each stall has its barker trying to lure you in. A whole meal costs about a pound and is a memorable experience.

The Zona Rosa is packed with restaurants—Japanese, Chinese, French, Spanish, Italian, German and yes, Mexican . . . you name it and you'll probably find it. Stroll down Calle Copenhague between Hamburgo and Paseo de la Reforma and you'll find an assortment of pavement restaurants. We particularly like **Mesón del Perro Andalúz** ('house of the Andalucian dog'), serving Spanish food. In the same block are the **Angus Steak House, El Perro d'Enfrente** (Italian), **El Chato** (Mexican), the **Picadilly Pub** and the **Verdi** (Mexican, international and pizza). One of our readers has recommended the **Salon Imperio** at Londres 132 as a good 'hole in the wall' restaurant serving a budget *comida corrida*.

The restaurant downstairs at the Museum of Anthropology in Chapultepec Park offers better service and food than might be expected in a museum restaurant.

Check the *Mexico City Daily Bulletin*, available at most hotels. Explore on your own, and chances are you'll come up with other great finds.

A word to the wise

Like most big cities, Mexico City is notorious for thievery, some of it most ingenious. Our friend Deborah was visiting the Metropolitan Cathedral when suddenly she was spattered with what appeared to be bird droppings. A solicitous Mexican appeared at her side and guided her over to the baptismal font, indicating that she should set her bag down while she used the holy water to clean up. A second man made off with her bag, and her helpful 'friend' energetically proclaimed his innocence.

Squirt guns full of bird droppings?

Keep your wits about you and seek the Golden Mean between foolhardiness and paranoia.

TOUR 1

EXPLORE MEXICO CITY

This tour will be devoted to exploring the sights of Chapultepec Park. *Chapultepec* is a Náhuatl Indian word meaning 'Grasshopper Hill'.

Suggested schedule

8:00	Breakfast at hotel. Those who want to take a guided tour to Teotihuacán tomorrow should arrange it through the hotel now.
9:00	Be at the Museum of Anthropology when it opens. Take an introductory tour and then explore at your leisure.
1:00	Lunch at the museum cafeteria.
1:30	Walk to Chapultepec Castle and take the tour.
3:00	Walk to the nearby Modern Art museum.
4:00	Cross the Reforma and see the Museo Rufina Tamayo. Or, if you're 'museumed out', stroll in the Zoo or return to your hotel early.
5:30	Return to the hotel.
7:00	Dinner. If you're still full of energy, explore the Zona Rosa or Garibaldi Plaza.

Sightseeing highlights

●●●**Museo Nacional de Antropología** (Museum of Anthropology)—Located in Paseo de la Reforma in Chapultepec Park, this museum is reason enough by itself to visit Mexico City. The handsome building houses 21 exhibition halls. The ground-floor halls cover the origins of human life in Meso-America and Mexico's ancient civilisations—Mexica (including Aztec), Toltec, Oaxaca, Gulf Coast and Maya. The first-floor halls show the cultures and life-styles of the many indigenous groups still living in Mexico today. Take a guided tour in English for a nominal fee (just wait for five people to gather). It lasts about 45 minutes and covers the Aztec and Teotihuacán civilisations. Buy a museum guidebook so you can locate those exhibits that interest you most. Panorama publishes a good one. Don't miss the outdoor reproduction of the Bonampak murals and the magnificent panels from Palenque in the Maya hall, or the reproduction of

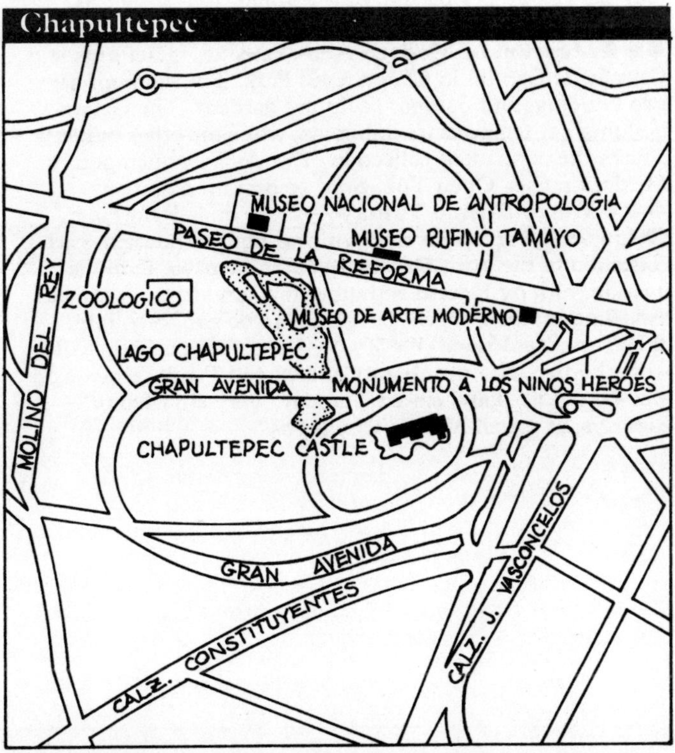

Monte Albán Tomb 104 in the Oaxaca hall. If you want supplementary guidebooks to any of the ruins on your itinerary, this is the place to buy them. Museum hours: open 9:00 a.m.-7:00 p.m. daily; closed Tuesday.

●●**Chapultepec Castle**—Built on the hilltop overlooking the park by the Viceroy Matias de Galvez in 1783, it later became a military academy. At the end of the Mexican War in 1847, six cadets died defending the castle from the U.S. Marines. The monument and massive pillars below commemorate these *Niños Héroes* (boy heroes).

The Emperor Maximilian and his wife Carlota lived here during their reign over Mexico. Walk around the terrace to the back of the building to see their restored furnished apartments. Be sure to see the Orozco mural in Sala 7. In the coach room, the coaches of Benito Juárez and Maximilian contrast the two leaders' lifestyles. You can take a 45-minute tour for £0.70p per person, or a 1½-hour tour for £1.35. Open Tue.-Sun. 9:00 a.m.-5:00 p.m.

●●●**Museum of Modern Art**—Paseo de la Reforma and Calzada de Gandhi in Chapultepec Park. The museum has two buildings and outdoor sculpture gardens. The Galería building has temporary exhibitions, while the other building houses the permanent collection of works by contemporary Mexican artists. Open Tue.-Sun. 10:00 a.m.-6:00 p.m.

●●●**Museo Rufino Tamayo**—Paseo de la Reforma in Chapultepec Park. This museum was built to house the art collection of the great Oaxacan painter Tamayo. Exhibits include work by Picasso and other modern artists, as well as travelling exhibits. Open Tue.-Sun. 10:00 a.m.-6:00 p.m.

●**Parque Zoológico** (the Zoo)—A must if you're travelling with children. See the Giant Condors and Panda. Open 9:00 a.m.-7:00 p.m. daily, closed Tuesday. Very crowded on Sundays, as are all Mexico City parks.

TOUR 2

MEXICO CITY AND TEOTIHUACÁN

This morning's walk will immerse you in the bustling life of central Mexico City. You'll spend the afternoon at the pre-Columbian pyramids of Teotihuacán, so mammoth that the Aztecs believed a race of giants had built them.

Suggested schedule

8:00	Enthusiastic sightseers have an early breakfast and sneak in a visit to the Merced Market.
9:00	The rest of us get up and have breakfast.
10:00	Begin walking tour with a stroll through Alameda Park.
12:30	Lunch.
1:30	Trip to the Teotihuacán pyramids. Optional to stay for dinner at the museum restaurant and the 7:00 p.m. sound and light show.
6:00	Those who've had enough, return to Mexico City.
7:00	Dinner. Collapse into bed, or . . .
9:00	Ballet Folklórico at the Bellas Artes.

Mercado Merced

This huge market, in the centre of old Mexico City, is easily reached by Metro. In fact, you can smell the vegetables of days gone by when you get off in the Merced station. If you love to eat, this is the most food you'll ever see under one roof! It's also a good chance to see the 'nitty gritty' side of Mexico City. The nearby Mercado Sonora (follow Avenida de Circumvalación to Fray Servando and turn left) has an awesome selection of ceramics, toys, miniatures, birds and witchcraft paraphernalia.

Central walking tour

Starting on the west end of Alameda Park, walk through the park to the domed Bellas Artes building. The Bellas Artes's exhibits include Diego Rivera's mural, *La Gran Victoria*. Pick up your tickets for the Ballet Folklórico if you're planning to go tonight. Leaving the Bellas Artes, turn left and then right to the Museo Nacional de Arte, at Tacuba 8.

Mexico City

Afterward walk back toward the Bellas Artes, turn left at Lázaro Cardénas, and notice the outrageous Post Office building. Turn left at Av. Madero and walk past the Casa de los Azulejos with its exterior of blue tiles, now a Sanborne's Restaurant. You will pass the Iglesia de San Francisco and the Iglesia de San Felipe de Jesús (*Iglesia* = church). In the next block on the right is the Palacio de Iturbide. Now a bank, its carved wooden doors are incredible. Peep in to see the wonderful stone pillared archways. You might want to browse in the American Bookstore at Madero 25. Further down you pass the Templo de la Profesa with its tower.

Arriving at the Zócalo, the Cathedral is on your left. Directly across from you is the Palacio Nacional (National Palace). The building on the far right houses offices of the Federal District. Go in and explore the impressive interior of the Cathedral. Next door is El Sagrario Metropolitano, orginally the private chapel of the viceroy.

Enter the National Palace and turn left up the stairway. You'll be greeted by a gigantic mural of the Spanish conquest and the fight for independence. On the first floor a beautiful Diego Rivera mural shows Aztec life before Cortés. Outside again, nip into the Zócalo Metro station and see the models of the Zócalo at various stages of its history.

Leaving the Metro, head back toward the Sagrario. To the

right you'll see a model of pre-Columbian Tenochtitlán. Walk through the ruins of the Templo Mayor.

Time for lunch!

Sightseeing highlights—central walking tour

●●●**Parque Alameda**—This beautiful park near the centre of Mexico City was created at the beginning of the seventeenth century. During its first 200 years, it was on the edge of the city.

●●●**Palacio de Bellas Artes** (Palace of Fine Arts) —Located at the east end of Alameda Park, this building is an extraordinary example of the late nineteenth century 'art nouveau' style. Construction was interrupted by the revolution of 1910, and the theatre was not completed until 1934. It is the home of the Ballet Folklórico and the National Symphony. To see the famous *cortina de cristales* (glass curtain) made of nearly a million pieces of stained glass and weighing 22 tons, you must attend a performance. The Bellas Artes museum has seven exhibition halls including murals by Rivera, Tamayo, Siqueiros and González Camereva. Open Tue.-Sun. 10:00 a.m.-6:30 p.m.

●●●**Museo Nacional de Arte**—Tacuba 8, across from the *Correos* (Post Office). The paintings by José María Velasco (1840-1912) are a fascinating record of the beautiful Valle de México as it was before the city ate it up. Notice how much of the great lake existed as late as the last century. Open Tue.-Sun. 10:00 a.m.-6:00 p.m.

●**Casa de los Azulejos** (House of Tiles)—Calle Madero 4. Built by the counts of the Valley of Orizaba, the interior with its tile-covered staircase and beautiful patio is now a popular restaurant and shops.

●●●**Plaza de la Constitución** *(El Zòcalo)*—The central plaza of Mexico City came to be called the Zócalo because a huge base for a statue (*zòcalo*) was built here in 1843, though the statue itself was never completed. The word *zòcalo* has come to mean central plaza throughout Mexico.

●●●**Catedral Metropolitana**—The largest religious building in the Americas, this magnificent cathedral was begun in 1567 and finished in 1813. Inside are five huge altars, fourteen side chapels and a black Christ known as *El Señor del Veneno*—The Lord of the Poison.

●●●**Palacio Nacional**—The National Palace was built in the sixteenth century on the site of Moctezuma's palace. It was the viceroy's residence in colonial times, and now houses the executive branch of the Mexican government, spectacular murals by Diego Rivera and a couple of dull museums.

Mexico's liberty bell adorns the central balcony.
●**Plaza de Garibaldi**—At the corner of Avenida Lazaro Cardenas and Calle Honduras, about ten minutes walk north from the Palacio Nacional. Mariachi bands gather here in the evening to play in the plaza or in nearby nightclubs. Besides mariachi bands (the ones with trumpets, violins and the huge bass guitar called *guitarón*) you'll hear norteño bands with accordion, and jarocho bands from Veracruz with huge harps. Motorists stop their cars along the main street passing the plaza for a few quick songs at the 'drive-in serenade'. The Bar Tenampa on this plaza serves a famous *ponche de grenada* (pomegranate punch).
●●●**Templo Mayor**—Ceremonial heart of the Aztec capital of Tenochtitlán, this pyramid over 150 feet high was destroyed by the *conquistadores*. On top of the pyramid were two temples dedicated to the gods Huitzilopochtli (war god) and Tlaloc (rain god). This ruin was discovered in 1978 by workers burying an underground cable. The famous Aztec Calendar Stone was found nearby in 1790.

The Pyramids of Teotihuacán

Teotihuacán is a Náhuatl Indian name meaning 'the place where gods were created'. This site dates back to 150 B.C., when the substructures of the Pyramids of the Sun and the Moon were built. According to legend, the fourth sun burned out before man existed. The gods gathered at Teotihuacán and decided that one of them should be sacrificed and turned into a Sun. Two of the gods leapt into the sacrificial flames and were transformed into the Sun and the Moon. It is estimated that the city of Teotihuacán flourished from about 100 B.C. to A.D. 700. The central axis of the ceremonial city runs north-south and was named The Avenue of the Dead by the Aztecs, based on their mistaken belief that the large mounds on either side were graves.

Getting there

Teotihuacán is located 32 miles north of Mexico City. Innumerable tours are available to the pyramids, competitively priced. Most leave in the morning, so you may wish to rearrange your schedule and do your central walk in late afternoon. Check with your hotel for tour information. Some pyramid tours include a visit to the famed Basílica de Guadalupe.

Getting to Teotihuacán by bus on your own is fairly simple. Take the Metro to station 'T.A. Norte' (for *Terminal de Autobuses Norte*). Once in the bus station, find the bus

Teotihuacán

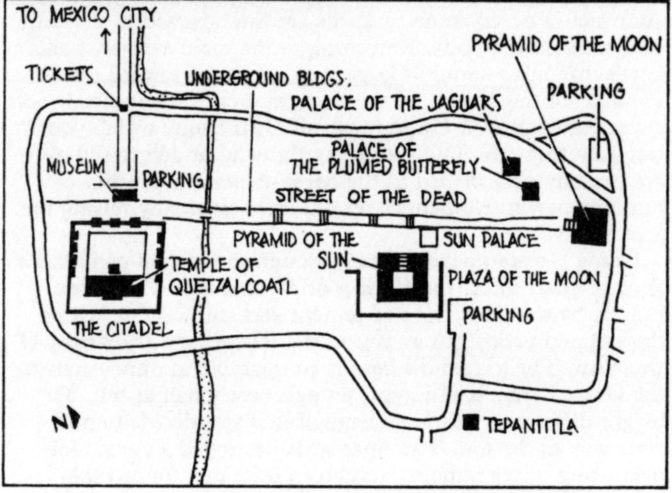

company called 'Mexico San Juan Teotihuacán Otumba Apam Capulalpan y Ramales, S.A. de C.V.'. The key word is Teotihuacán, and you'll find the ticket office near the big green and white sign that says 'Espera 8' (Waiting Room 8). Buses leave every half-hour from 7:00 a.m. to 3:00 p.m. The trip takes about an hour. Don't miss the last bus back at 6:00 p.m. The bus drops you off on the road at the cobbled driveway leading to the museum entrance, and picks up returning passengers at the same spot.

A reader suggests that an easier way to get to Teotlhuacán is by taking the Metro to Indios Verdes station and catching a bus from there, but we haven't tried it.

Walk through the Ruins

Start at the **Museum**, with its reproduction of the water goddess Chalchiuhtlicue (the first of a long series of Aztec and Mayan tongue twisters). See the wall paintings collected from various temples.

Directly opposite the museum is **The Citadel** (*La Ciudadela*). Excavation revealed that this superstructure covers an older, much more impressive and ornate monument, **The Temple of Quetzalcoátl**, now partially revealed at the rear of the complex. Built between A.D. 200 and 250, this pyramid is adorned with sculptured heads of the feathered serpent Quetzalcoátl and another more stylised figure, identified as either the rain god Tlaloc or the corn god. Take your pick. Carved stone seashells are interspersed in the coils of Quetzalcoátl's body. Returning to the main avenue, walk north through a series of large stepped patios toward the Pyramid of the Moon. In the first patio on the left metal roofs cover the excavated **Underground Buildings,** which you can walk through. They weren't originally underground, of course, but were buried in the Meso-American practice of building new monuments over old ones, gradually raising the ground level.

Patios 2-5 are unexceptional, though the second patio has a floor of sheet mica (the **Viking** or **Mica Floor Complex**) hidden by the thick floor of cement and stucco. The last of the stepped patios brings you to the **Plaza and Pyramid of the Sun**. The pyramid's base is comparable in dimensions to the Great Pyramid of Egypt, though barely half as tall. The height difference will seem negligible if you decide to puff your way to the top. The Spaniards destroyed a stone idol measuring 'three fathoms' (eighteen feet) that topped this temple. **The Palace of the Sun** lies in front of and slightly north of the pyramid.

Continuing north toward the Pyramid of the Moon, you will see a shed roof on the right which protects the remains of a mural painting of a jaguar. When you get to the **Plaza of the Moon**, turn sharp left at the corner and go up the steps of the **Palace of the Plumed Butterfly** (Quetzalpapalotl). At the top of the stairway, on the north side (in front of the pillared hall containing the remains of murals in red) is a huge serpent's head. The inner courtyard has pillars adorned with the mythological butterfly that gives this palace its endearing name. Some decorative obsidian disks remain in the bas-reliefs.

Retracing your steps, leave the palace and turn right. A narrow stairway terminates in a large courtyard, the **Palace of the Jaguars**. Built in A.D. 450-650, this building features murals of a jaguar either blowing into or drinking out of a feathered conch. As you leave this courtyard, a modern tunnel to the right leads you into the **Substructure of the Feathered Shells** built in the second and third centuries A.D. Located under the Quetzal-butterfly's palace, this temple is adorned with bas-relief sculptures of feathered conches with mouthpieces, presumed to have been musical instruments, and four-petalled flowers. A low platform decorated with murals of green birds, best seen on the way out on the south-east side, supports the temple. Leaving this complex of buildings, return to the Plaza of the Moon and gird yourself for another *subida y bajada* (ascent and descent). **The Pyramid of the Moon,** composed of four huge sloping terraces, ends our walk up this grand road.

But you're not finished yet! If you've got it in you, it's worth a side trip on your way back to see **Tepantitla,** with its remains of the mural of the **Paradise of Tlaloc,** depicting human figures at play, chasing butterflies and bathing. To get there, turn left just north of the Pyramid of the Sun. Walk through Car Park No. 2 and down the road linking it to Tepantitla, about half a mile from the main avenue. (Out of energy? You can see a reproduction of the mural in the museum.)

It takes three hours at a brisk trot to see the Teotihuacán ruins. Add 45 minutes for each pyramid climb. Of course, you may want to linger longer, or take a few minutes to buy a dozen clay whistles and a couple of crystal balls. (Vendors swarm here like mosquitoes.)

TOUR 3

MEXICO CITY—SAN MIGUEL

Today you'll leave Mexico City for the beautiful old hill town of San Miguel de Allende, the adopted home of many foreign artists and expatriates. You'll spend the afternoon enjoying the shops, parks and narrow cobbled streets of this colonial town.

Suggested schedule

9:00	Leave Mexico City.
1:00	Arrive in San Miguel de Allende, get settled in your hotel and have lunch.
3:00	Sit in the plaza, locally known as the *jardin* (garden), and people-watch. Slip into the Parroquía and San Rafael churches.
4:00	Explore some of the craft shops and boutiques.
5:00	Walking tour 1.
7:00	Dinner. Afterward, sample San Miguel's nightlife.

Transport: Mexico City-San Miguel de Allende (180 miles)

By car: If you hire a car in Mexico City for this part of the trip, do so at the airport. There is a large selection of car-hire firms at the airport and you'll avoid driving in the centre of Mexico City. You'll leave the city on motorways and connect with toll road 57-D toward Querétaro. Ask at the airport tourist information booth for directions to the car-hire area. The hire company will provide maps and directions to Querétaro. When you reach Querétaro, follow the signs for San Luis Potosí to bypass the city. Fifteen to twenty minutes past Querétaro a sign marks the turn-off to San Miguel de Allende.

By bus: Take a taxi to the Terminal del Norte bus station. Two first-class companies serve San Miguel: Tres Estrellas de Oro and Omnibus de Mexico. Second-class companies are Flecha Amarilla and Herradura de Plata. Find the ticket office for one of these bus companies and buy your ticket. Services are frequent, so one of them should have a bus just ready to leave. The trip takes about 4 hours.

Orientation—San Miguel de Allende

In the mid-sixteenth century, San Miguel was a Spanish military outpost and the site of a mission founded by Fray Juan de San Miguel. It was incorporated as a town in 1555, and took its present name, San Miguel de Allende, from the revolutionary hero born here. Once a compact colonial hill town, San Miguel is fast sprawling in all directions. Fortunately, the Mexican government has preserved the timeless charm of the city centre by declaring it a national historic monument.

San Miguel's two art schools, the Instituto Allende and Bellas Artes, have attracted foreign students for the past forty years, and many have stayed. To see why, wander around and discover handsome colonial facades, a balcony wild with geraniums or your own favourite crooked little alley.

The state of Guanajuato has been a rich mining area since colonial times, producing great quantities of silver, opal, fire agate, amethyst and other gemstones. Silverwork and high-quality jewellery can be found in the shops of San Miguel. There is also metalwork in brass and tin, including elaborate and ornate mirror frames, glass boxes and lampshades. There is textile work in wool and cotton, and in San Miguel you can buy heavy wool sweaters and jackets knitted by jail inmates. The handsome and fanciful tiles produced in the town of Dolores Hidalgo, available in San Miguel, may tempt you to load up an extra suitcase to do your bathroom or kitchen.

Walking tour 1

This one's for mountain goats, so if you're feeling lazy or creaky spend the time exploring shops, then take a taxi to El Mirador just before sunset.

Follow Cuna Allende street (on the west side of the Parroquía), until it becomes Aldama and leads you right into Parque Benito Juárez, known locally as 'French Park'. Hopefully the lilies will be in bloom. Rest near a fountain or watch youngsters on the basketball courts.

Walk diagonally through the park and then up the hill to the left, past the public *pilas* where women wash clothes. Inhale deeply, then proceed up the steep zigzag cobblestone walkway of El Chorro (the 'spurt' or 'stream', originally a public bathhouse). Take the stairs to the front of the Capilla de la Santa Cruz del Chorro and continue ever upward on the cobbled alley to your right. Little Callejón del Chorro brings you to the road to Querétaro, just above El Mirador, a great spot for a panoramic photo.

San Miguel

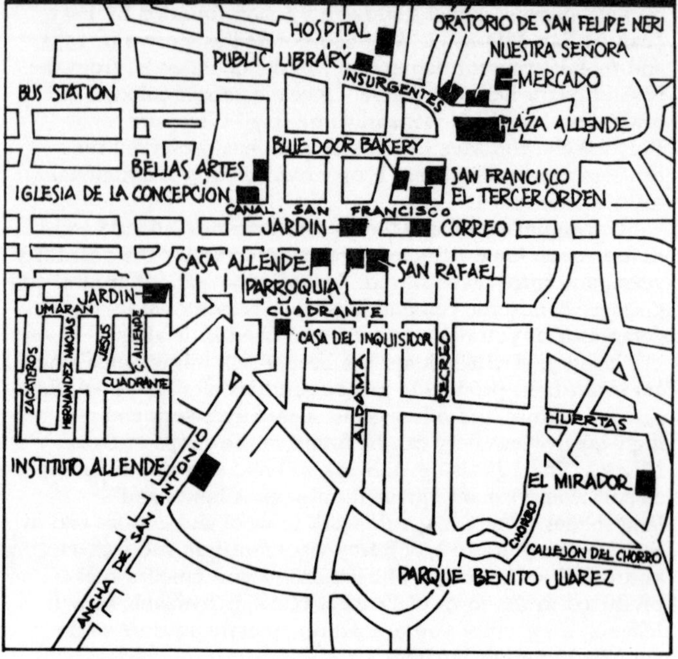

San Miguel is dear to painters and photographers for its exquisite quality of light. After the spectacular *puesta del sol* (sunset), walk downhill and turn left into the second alleyway, Callejón de las Huertas. Continue downhill, turn right into Recreo and follow your map to San Francisco Church. Then go on to the Oratorio de San Felipe Neri to see the ornate chapel of La Santa Casa de Loreto.

Sightseeing highlights—walking tour 1

●●●**La Parroquía** (the parish church)—The original simple church was built in the seventeenth century by architect Marcos Antonio Sobrarias. The ornate facade was added in the late 1880s by mason Ceferino Gutiérrez who, so the story goes, copied a cathedral from a European postcard. This lovely building is in the centre of town and its Gothic pink spires dominate the skyline.

●**San Rafael**—The most notable feature of this simple church is a series of life-size dioramas depicting the crucifixion and scourging of Christ.

●●**San Francisco Church**—The churrigueresque exterior contrasts with the serene and austere lines of the pink stone interior.

●●●**Oratorio de San Felipe Neri** and **La Santa Casa de Loreto**—The marvellous towers and cupolas of this church add grace to San Miguel's skyline. The church houses the remarkable Santa Casa de Loreto, the original private chapel of the *condes* (colonial nobility). The chapel's floor and walls are covered in tiles from China, Valencia and Puebla. This is one of the most truly ornate chapels in Mexico, unique for its goldwork over carved stone rather than the traditional wood.

Accommodation

San Miguel has a great diversity of hotels and inns, with a wide range of prices.

For a treat, **Hotel Posada La Ermita** (Calle Real de Querétaro 64, tel. 2-07-77) has spacious rooms with *salas* (sitting rooms) and balconies. This hotel is on a hilltop, with lots of stairs, and has a swimming pool. We like **Hotel Mansión del Bosque** (Aldama 65, tel. 2-02-72, write or phone ahead for reservations)—charming, two meals included.

Moderately priced bed and breakfast is available in the off seasons (spring and autumn) at **Posada Casa Carmen**, a pretty colonial hotel (Correo 31, tel. 20-84-4). In winter or summer you need reservations and lodging comes higher-priced with three meals daily. Other moderate hotels are the **Hotel San Francisco** right on the plaza (Plaza Principal 2, tel. 2-00-72), and **Posada de las Monjas** (Canal 37, tel. 2-01-71). Or try the **Mesón San Antonio** (Mesones 80).

Our favourite budget hotel is the **Hotel Sebastián** (Mesones 7), which has big clean rooms, most with fireplaces—San Miguel can be chilly in the winter. The **Hotel Sautto** (59 Hernandez Macias, tel. 2-00-52) is a budget hotel boasting a lovely garden courtyard.

Food

With the exception of Mexico City, San Miguel is arguably the best eating town in Mexico. Thanks to the large foreign population and weekend migrations of *chilangos* (slightly impolite name for people from Mexico City), there are many speciality restaurants you wouldn't expect to find in a small Mexican town. Besides excellent Mexican cuisine you'll find everything from pizza to Chinese food.

For the best food in town and a very special atmosphere, we highly recommend **Restaurant Virginia** at Mesones 95, inside the patio and upstairs. She has a Tuesday Special of international cuisine and also features homemade pastries, ice cream, and other take-away delicacies. Happy hour 6:00-8:00 p.m. with tasty snacks, homemade pizza. The restaurant is also a gallery, featuring Virginia's designer clothes, colourful tapestry rugs and paintings by local artist Margit Ilika.

Though more expensive than Restaurant Virginia, locals also recommend **La Jacaranda** at Aldama 53 for gourmet cuisine. The restaurant-bar **La Bugumbilla** (Hidalgo 42) has been around San Miguel for years in various locations. It serves well-prepared regional dishes as well as an international menu. A newer establishment with similar menu is **Restaurant La Casona** (Canal 21) in the Bazar Plaza Colonial. The service is particularly good here and the food has always been good, too: there's a bar. For diehard carnivores lusting for a large steak, we suggest **Juan's Steak House** on the Salida de Querétaro on the left as you're going out of town. The menu consists almost entirely of steaks (the best we've had in Mexico), served with tossed salad and chips.

For more economical eating, we like **La Casita** (Hernández Macías 85), a pleasant place for lunch. Try the chicken soup! Another good place for a full meal or a quick snack is the **Café Colón** (San Francisco 21). The service is fast, the food is good and the price is right. For a wonderfully old-fashioned atmosphere (walls hand-painted to look like wallpaper), enjoy a meal at **Caféteria El Correo**, Correo 23.

For a real cup of coffee, espresso or *cappuccino*, drop into the **Parroquiano-Casa de Té y Café** (Insurgentes 74, across from the public library). They have excellent desserts, breakfasts, and reasonably priced entrées. A good cup of coffee can also be found in the folk art store **Pegasus** across the street from the post office in Correo—they have a beautiful folk art collection, too. Another popular spot for a cup of good coffee is **La Dolce Vita** in the Bazar Plaza Colonial on Canal. For sweet treats and delicious whole wheat bread, don't miss the **Blue Door Bakery** (otherwise known as La Colmena) at Reloj 21.

San Miguel nightlife

A popular and pleasant place to hear good music and perhaps eat a late supper is **Mama Mia's** (Umarán 8, just down from the plaza). The music is usually better than the food, but the pizza is quite acceptable and the service, though slow, is friendly. With luck you may hear the excellent Spanish flamenco music played by Wolf and Diana. At other times a Mexican group plays Andean music as well as traditional Mexican music, salsa and rock (sometimes all at the same time!).

For everything from American country and western to jazz, try **Pancho and Lefty's** (Mesones 99, closed Mondays), serving drinks and light food. You can dance there, and sometimes things get pretty wild. San Miguel's expatriate meeting place, **La Fragua** (Cuna de Allende 3) has a happy hour from 6:00 to 8:00 p.m., with live music thereafter. Clifford Irving often uses this bar as a setting in his novels. **La Princesa** (in Recreo just up from the post office) features Mexican popular music most nights and stays open late. Or for reggae, rock and salsa, try **El Borolote** (Calle de Jesus 25), open Thu., Fri., and Sat. For disco dancing, try **The Ring** on Hidalgo between Insurgentes and Mesones or **Los Laberintos** on the Salida a Celaya.

We highly recommend María de Cespede's **Athanor Theatre Company** for magical performances at Mesones 5 most Friday and Saturday evenings.

Helpful hints

The local bilingual newspaper *Atención San Miguel* comes out on Thursday and is a good source of information on current art and music events. Available at the library, in supermarkets and at El Colibrí bookstore (Sollano 30, has books in English and art supplies).

For additional information on San Miguel, visit the tourist office on the east side of the Parroquía near the Terraza restaurant. Open Mon.-Fri. 10:00 a.m.-2.45 p.m. and 5:00-7:00 p.m., Sat. 10:00 a.m.-1:00 p.m., Sun. 10:00 a.m.-Noon.

The *Biblioteca Pública* (public library) at Insurgentes 25 has books, magazines and newspapers in English, and you're welcome to go in and read them. Open Mon.-Sat. 10:00 a.m.-2:00 p.m., 4:00-7:00 p.m.

La Luciernega, on Aldama near Cuadrante, develops film and has a quick postal service for letters home for a small fee.

TOUR 4

SAN MIGUEL DE ALLENDE

Today you'll sightsee around town and then visit an unusual penitent church. You'll then enjoy a delicious picnic lunch and soak your weary bones in the hot springs of Las Grutas.

Suggested schedule

8:00	Breakfast.
9:00	Walking tour 2.
1:00	Bus, taxi or drive to Atotonilco.
2:00	To Las Grutas. Soak, swim and picnic.
5:00	Return to town, relax before dinner.
6:00	Happy hour and dinner. Go out and listen to music or curl up in bed with a book.

Walking tour 2

Walk down Calle Canal on the right-hand side where you have a better view of the handsome Casa de Mayorazgo de Canal on the north-west corner. Turn right into Hernández Macías and go into the Bellas Artes. See the adjoining Iglesia de la Concepción. (Detour: flea market buffs may want to check out the San Miguel Tuesday Market. Follow Canal to the bottom of the hill, and you'll see an outdoor market on your right.)

Continue down Canal and turn left onto Zacateros, which takes you to Calle Ancha de San Antonio and the Instituto Allende. Visit the galleries, then walk back to town along Hernández Macías to Cuadrante. Turn right to pass the Casa del Carcél de la Inquisición on the corner. Turn left into Jesús and follow your map back to the *jardin*. Go into the Casa de Allende. Cross the square and go down Reloj. The building decorated with gargoyles and Stars of David is the Casa Cohen. Let the fragrance of the Blue Door Bakery seduce you into some *pan dulces* (sweet rolls) for your picnic lunch.

Reloj will lead you to Insurgentes and, turning right, you can walk up through the outdoor street market. Notice the market's own shrine to the Virgin on the corner.

Stop in at the Iglesia de la Salud in Green Horse Square. (If you don't see a green horse, it's because the statue was moved to El Mirador for some mysterious reason. Locals still call this the Green Horse Square anyway.) On the east side of the square, turn left to get to the indoor market.

At a stand, have sandwiches made up for your picnic or, if you prefer, pick up some *carnitas* (barbecued pork) sandwiches at Apollo 11 over in Mesones.

Sightseeing highlights—walking tour 2

●●**Casa de Allende**—This former home of the revolutionary hero Ignacio de Allende has recently been restored and turned into a museum. It has not yet established a permanent collection but has rotating monthly exhibits. Open Tue.-Sat. 10:00 a.m.-5:00 p.m., Sun. 10:00 a.m.-3:00 p.m., closed Mon.

●**El Tercer Orden**—The oldest church in San Miguel, built in 1713.

●●**Nuestra Senora de la Salud**—This simple church façade is capped by a large seashell design. Notice the collection of prayers, photos and *milagros* (lit. 'miracles', small metal amulets) inside in front of the statue of the Niño de la Salud, evidence of healings, blessings and prayers answered.

●●●**Iglesia de la Concepción**—The church was built between 1755 and 1765, and its cupola, designed by the same mason who did the Parroquía, was added in 1891. The interior of the church is of *cantera rosa* (rose-pink stone) and has a large gold-leafed altar-piece. Peep into the chapel behind the choir grille for a glimpse of the private chapel of the nunnery.

●●●**Bellas Artes**—This art school is housed in the former Convent of the Church of the Concepción. Directly on the right as you enter is a bulletin board with announcements of current art exhibitions and concerts. There is a gallery on the left and a second gallery diagonally across the courtyard. In the little coffee shop attached to the second gallery you'll see the Pedro Martinez mural 'La Pulquería' ('The Pulque Shop'. Pulque is an alcoholic beverage made from the maguey plant). The galleries are open 10:00 a.m.-2:00 p.m. and 4:00-7:30 p.m. weekdays.

●●●**Instituto Allende**—Founded in 1951, this art school occupies the former house of the Mayorazgo de la Canal. The history of the Instituto is on a display board in the entrance. To the right is a bulletin board with a schedule of classes and notices of current events. There are two galleries: one displays works by painter James Pinto, the other rotating exhibits. To get to the galleries, turn left at the entrance and walk around the courtyard past the coffee shop and murals. Gallery hours are Mon.-Fri. 10:00 a.m.-1:00 p.m. and 3:00-6:00 p.m., Sat. 10:00 a.m.-Noon.

Atotonilco

A bus marked *Santuario* leaves on the hour from the south-east corner of Green Horse Square at the sign *Parada de Urbanos* (cleverly concealed by the 'Farmacia San Miguel' sign). The ride takes about half an hour.

The Sanctuary of Atotonilco and House of Spiritual Exercises was built between 1740 and 1802. Its interior is entirely covered with murals of angels and devils, flowers, leaves, fruits and mystical poems. Atotonilco attracts droves of pilgrims each year. Some penitents attempt to expiate their sins by wearing crowns of thorns and whipping themselves in imitation of Christ. Two weeks before Easter every year thousands of Mexicans walk in candlelit procession from the Sanctuary to San Miguel carrying the statue of Nuestro Señor de la Columna, arriving in the town at dawn. Buses return to San Miguel every hour. Catch one heading back to town and get off at Manatiales de las Grutas.

Las Grutas

A number of natural hot springs around San Miguel have been developed as bathing spots. We find Las Grutas the most pleasant. Besides a big swimming pool, it offers a series of pools of graduated temperatures. The last and hottest pool is inside an artificial cave. During the summer all the lawns are green and you can eat bananas and figs from the plants overhanging the pools. Manatiales de las Grutas is open daily, 8:00-5:00, and costs about £1.30 per person.

Flag down any bus on the main road to get a ride back to town.

TOUR 5

SAN MIGUEL-GUANAJUATO

Today you'll leave San Miguel for Guanajuato. You'll have fun testing your wits against the underground streets and meandering alleyways of the city as you visit the sights. This is the place to explore on your own.

Suggested schedule

8:00	Leave for Guanajuato.
9:30	Arrive in Guanajuato and check into a hotel. If you want a tour this afternoon, go to the tour office and sign up.
10:30	Begin walking tour 1 at the Basílica on Avenida Juárez.
1:00	Lunch.
2:00	Visit the market.
2:30	Walk 2, starting from the market.
3:30	Hire a taxi at El Pípila for further sightseeing, or return to town in time to catch your tour.
7:00	Dinner.
8:00	Drinks and people-watching in Jardín Unión.

Transport

Catch a Flecha Amarilla ('Yellow Arrow') bus from San Miguel to Guanajuato at the new bus station on the outskirts of town about 8:00 a.m. You will probably want to take a taxi to the bus station. Or you can leave town in style by taking a taxi from San Miguel to Guanajuato for £10–£15.

Drivers—head out of town toward Celaya. Several miles out of town, turn right following the sign to Guanajuato. Once you get to Guanajuato you're on your own—there's no way we could possibly explain how to get around Guanajuato by car.

Orientation

The elegant Jardín Unión in the centre of Guanajuato belies the city's origins as a rough and ready mining town. Founded in 1557 to strip the earth of its incredibly rich silver deposits, the town grew along a canyon and up the sides of the surrounding hills. Some of the streets run underground through old mine tunnels and the former riverbed, creating an

Guanajuato

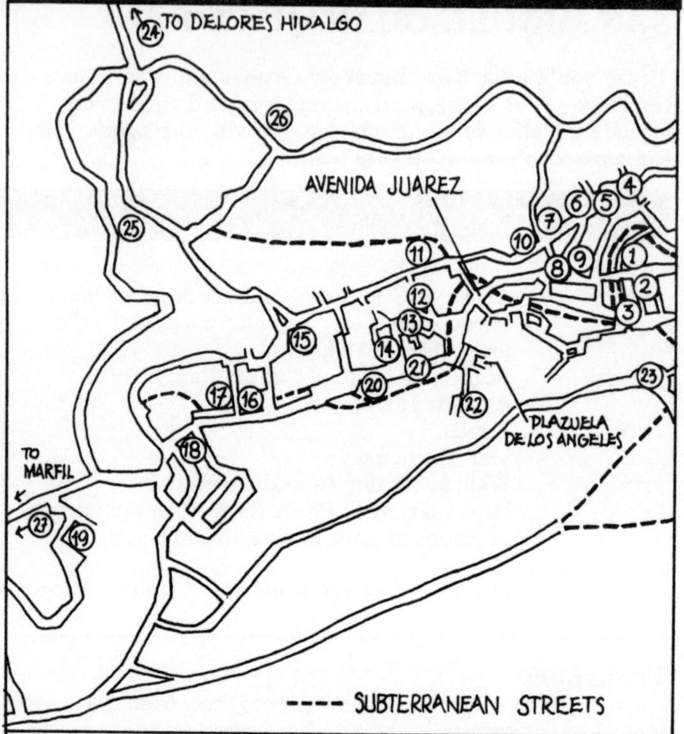

① JARDÍN UNIÓN ② TEATRO JUÁREZ ③ TEMPLO DE SAN DIEGO ④ PLAZUELA DEL BARATILLO ⑤ CORREO ⑥ TEMPLO DE LA COMPANÍA ⑦ UNIVERSIDAD DE GUANAJUATO ⑧ PLAZA DE LA PAZ ⑨ BASILICA DE NUESTRA SENORA DE GUANAJUATO ⑩ MUSEO DE PUEBLO DE GUANAJUATO ⑪ MUSEO DIEGO RIVERA ⑫ PLAZUELA DE SAN FERNANDO ⑬ PLAZUELA DE SAN ROQUE ⑭ PLAZA DE LA REFORMA (JARDIN MORELOS) ⑮ ALHÓNDIGA DE GRANADITAS ⑯ TOURIST OFFICE ⑰ BUS STATION ⑱ HOSPITAL ⑲ LAS MOMIAS (MUMMIES) ⑳ MERCADO HIDALGO ㉑ LA PURISIMA (BAKERY) ㉒ CALLEJON DEL BESO ㉓ EL PIPILA ㉔ IGLESIA Y MINA LA VALENCIANA ㉕ MUSEO DE MINAS ㉖ IGLESIA DE LA CATA ㉗ EX-HACIENDA DE SAN GABRIEL BARRERA

incredibly complicated labyrinth. Its famous Granary Building is the site of one of the first battles in the Revolution for independence from Spain. Shortly thereafter the Spaniards hung the heads of the leading insurgents on hooks at the four corners of the building, where they were displayed for ten years.

Guanajuato (which means 'Many frogs that sing in the water') has a very European air, and in its many streets and alleys you would swear you had stepped into Italy. This is the ideal city to get lost in, and you probably will. Small alleyways and staircases open invitingly off the many intimate plazas, and the verb *callejonear* (to alley-walk) may well have been invented here. Whenever you find yourself lured off into unknown regions (lost!) just walk downhill and you'll find the *centro* again.

Guanajuato is famous (or infamous) for its mummies, which you may or may not wish to visit, and for its International Cervantino Festival in mid-October. People from all over the world attend the Festival plays and concerts. If you'll be there at Festival time, make hotel reservations six months in advance.

Accommodation

The most deluxe central hotel is the **Posada Santa Fe**, located in the *jardín* (Jardín Unión 12, tel. 2- 00-84, 2-02-07); you usually need reservations one month in advance. Equally attractive is the **Hotel San Diego**, also in the square at Jardín Unión 1 (tel. 2-13-00).

Our favourite moderate hotel is the **Hacienda de Cobros**, near the bus station (Juárez 153, tel. 2-01-43). Our second choice is the **Mineral de Rayas** (Calle Alhóndiga 7, tel. 2-19-67). For budget travellers we recommend the **Hotel Central** (Juárez 11, tel. 2-00-80) or the **Hotel Posada San Francisco** at the Plaza de Gavira, off Avenida Juárez near the market.

Food

The restaurant at the **Posada Santa Fe** has been written up in *Gourmet* magazine; it's a little expensive. The **Restaurant Valadez**, also in the *jardín*, has a moderately priced and tasty *comida corrida*.

Steve highly recommends the **Tasca de los Santos**, a Spanish restaurant in Plaza de la Paz 28 across from the Basílica. There's good barbecued chicken at **La Carreta**, Juárez 96. Tina likes **El Claustro** in the Jardín Morelos, a good lunch stop after walking tour 1; you eat in the kitchen.

The **Bar Luna** has pavement tables on the *jardín* and good drinks. Try the Sangria, but watch out—it's stronger than it tastes.

Getting around

The main artery of the town is Avenida Juárez, which runs from the mummies past the market and Basílica to the central plaza and beyond.

Tours: Transportes Turísticos de Guanajuato at Bajo Basílica 2 (in Avenida Juárez just below the Basílica) has tours at 10:15 a.m. and 4:00 p.m.—if at least ten people are signed up. The tour bus will pick you up at your hotel if you make arrangements when you make your reservation. Tours are in Spanish unless you happen to get the one English-speaking driver. Steve calls this tour a totally Mexican experience, and very entertaining. The tour is supposed to last 3½ hours but may take as long as 5½ hours. Included are the mummies, El Pípila and a drive around the Panorámica, the village and church of Mineral de Cata and the Church of Valenciana. (Tel. 2-21-34 or 2-37-64.)

Taxis: If you prefer hiring a taxi to taking the tour, we suggest you include the ex-Hacienda de San Gabriel Barrera and the Mining Museum. You can negotiate a taxi for £2–£3 per hour.

Walking tour 1

Start walking at the Basílica on Avenida Juárez. Turn left out of the church and walk up Juárez to the Templo de San Diego on your right, facing onto the Jardín Unión, the central plaza. Visit Teatro Juárez right next door. Turning right as you leave, follow Avenida Juárez about 200 yards to the Cervantes Museum, on your right. After visiting the museum, retrace your steps to the *jardín*. Walk through this small elegant plaza to the Posada Santa Fe and turn right onto the mall leading out of the plaza.

Take the first left (in front of the Pizza Piazza) into the Plazuela del Baratillo. Passing the fountain, follow the alleyway on the left to the Plaza de Compañía. This is a good time to buy stamps or post letters at the *Correos* (post office) on the corner. Go into the Templo de la Compañía across the street. Continue on to view the unusual University building. On the right just past the University is the Museo del Pueblo de Guanajuato. Continue along Pocitos until you come to the Casa de Diego Rivera.

After visiting this museum continue in the same direction, turning at the first left and an immediate second left that leads down to the Plazuela de San Fernando. The second exit on the right leads into the Plazuela de San Roque, equipped with benches and lighting for plays during the Cervantes festival. Cross the plaza and go downstairs into Jardín Morelos (also known as the Plaza de la Reforma). Walk through the archway into Juárez, turn right and then right again up the hill into Calle de Granaditas. The first left leads you to the Alhóndiga de Granaditas on the left.

Sightseeing highlights—walking tour 1

●●●**Basílica de Nuestra Señora de Guanajuato**—The seventeenth-century baroque-style cathedral houses the 1,300-year-old statue, originally from Spain, of the Virgin Mary, patron saint of the city. The huge crystal chandelier over the altar is locally known as *La Araña* (the spider). The church is located in the Plaza de Paz (Peace Square).

●**Templo de San Diego**—The small churrigueresque style church next to Teatro Juárez on the Jardín Unión dates from the 18th century.

●●●**Teatro Juárez**—Completed in 1903 during the presidency of Porfirio Diáz, the beautiful Moorish theatre's façade is embellished with Doric columns and statues. In the Jardín Unión.

Museo Cervantes—A reader recommends this delightful world-class museum with two floors of paintings, prints and sculpture devoted to Don Quixote and Sancho Panza.

●●●**Templo de la Compañía**—This beautiful old church, built by the Jesuits, was completed in 1765. The elaborately carved churrigueresque façade makes it the most spectacular of Guanajuato's 28 Catholic churches. (Aren't you glad you're only visiting five?)

●**The University of Guanajuato** is considered one of the best universities in Mexico. The unusual building looks old but was completed in 1955.

●**Museo del Pueblo de Guanajuato** (Museum of the People of Guanajuato)—Located in the home of the Marques de San Juan Rayas, built in 1776, the museum has art exhibits, historical displays and murals by José Chávez Morado. Open Tue.-Sat. 10:00 a.m.-noon and 4:00-7:00 p.m., Sun. 10:00 a.m.-4:00 p.m.

●●**Museo Diego Rivera**—The lower floor is a reconstruction of the home where Rivera lived until age six. Exhibits of some of his early work are on the upper two floors. Open Mon.-Sat. 10:00 a.m.-2:00 p.m. and 4:00-7:00 p.m., Sun. 10:00 a.m.-4:00 p.m.

●●●**Alhóndiga de Granaditas**—Completed in 1809 as

the city granary, this fortress-like building became famous as the place where the first battle for independence from Spain was won by insurgents Hidalgo, Ignacio Allende, Mariano Jiménez and Juan Aldama. Here El Pípilo, an Indian miner, set the door of the Alhóndiga on fire, allowing the insurgents to enter and rout the Spaniards holed up inside. Today the Alhóndiga is the Regional State Museum. There are many interesting exhibits of local history as well as an exhibition of arts and crafts from the state of Guanajuato. Open Tue.-Sat. 10:00 a.m.-2:00 p.m. and 4:00-7:00 p.m., Sun. 10:00 a.m.-4:00 p.m.

Walking tour 2

This is a *subida* (hill climb). You may wish to take a taxi instead to El Pípila and on to the itinerary suggested under 'Getting Around: Taxis'.

Turn right as you leave the market and walk up Juárez to the Plazuela de Los Angeles. Take the first right into Callejón del Patrocinio, which is marked Callejonear Ruta 2. Take the first left into Callejón del Beso (so called because lovers leaning from one balcony to the other can kiss across the alley). Turn left, following the Ruta 2 sign, at the next corner. Walk down to Posada de los Angeles and turn right going uphill. At a rust-red coloured house with many pots of geraniums and ferns, turn right. At this point you're going up Callejón de la Barranca. Just before the alley appears to end in a private home, there's a turn to the right—take it. Past the *tienda* (store), turn left at the raised flower garden on your right, and continue up the obvious walkway to El Pípila. Three gold stars if you made it without getting lost!

Sightseeing highlights—walking tour 2 and afternoon tour

●●●**Mercado Hidalgo**—This market, in a metal building that looks like an old aeroplane hangar, features Day of the Dead sweets (in shapes of skeletons) year-round. Food is downstairs, *artesanías* (folk arts, handicrafts) upstairs.

●**El Pípila**—Located on a *mirador* (viewpoint) on the Carretera Panorámica, the big ugly statue of Juan José de los Reyes Martinez is better known as El Pípila. You came for the magnificent view.

●●●**La Iglesia de la Valenciana** (Templo de San Cayetano)—Built in 1788. It is said that the Count of Valenciana, owner of the nearby mine, required workers in the mine to contribute 'a handful of ore a week' toward the building of the church; then he got the credit! The interior is graced with three huge altar pieces elaborately carved and finished in 24 ct gold. The pulpit of mahogany is inlaid with ivory and tortoiseshell.

●●●**La Valenciana Mine**—One of the richest mines in history is now working again after being closed for years. It has attractive park-like grounds and a shop where you can buy silver jewellery. Take a look at the huge pit where ore is brought up to be sent to the smelter at La Cata. Beautiful quartz crystals and other minerals are sold at shops in the nearby village.

●●●**Ex-Hacienda de San Gabriel Barrera**—This elegant hacienda and extensive formal gardens adjacent to the Hotel Presidente on the road to Marfil was a private home until Mrs. Lopez Portillo, wife of the President, donated it to the state in 1976. The rooms are beautifully restored with their original furniture.

●●**El Museo de Minería** (Mining Museum)—A rock-lover's heaven! Two floors of glass cases filled with incredible crystals, mineral specimens, fossils and cut gemstones. The museum is at the Escuela de Minas y Metalurgia (School of Mines and Metallurgy) on the road toward Dolores Hidalgo.

●**Iglesia de la Cata**—Located at Mineral la Cata above the city. Completed in 1725 and known as the miners' church, it has a beautiful carved stone façade. Inside, the walls are covered with *retablos*—primitive drawings and descriptions of miracles answering prayers.

●**Las Momias** (The Mummies)—A distasteful display of naturally mummified cadavers removed from the local cemetery because the rent on their graves was unpaid (the ultimate eviction). Some of the mummies have been on display for over 100 years. They are a popular tourist attraction. See them, if you must, at the *panteón* (cemetery).

TOUR 6

GUANAJUATO—PÁTZCUARO

Today you will depart from Guanajuato, with its distinctly European flavour, to enter a whole new world—that of the Tarascan Indians of Pátzcuaro. In the afternoon you'll take an easy walk around town to see some of the sights and absorb the atmosphere of this 'laid-back' lake town.

Suggested schedule

8:00	Early bird departure from Guanajuato for Pátzcuaro by way of Morelia.
1:00	Lunch in Morelia in the central plaza or near bus station.
2:00	Continue on to Pátzcuaro by bus or car.
3:00	Check into your hotel.
4:00	Take a gentle walk to visit the sights of Pátzcuaro.
6:00	Dinner. There isn't a lot to do here at night, so this is a good time to write some letters, catch up with your diary or practise your tai chi.

Transport

Bus travellers: Back on the Yellow Arrow (Flecha Amarilla), the only bus service from Guanajuato to Morelia in the morning. Buses leave on the hour from 6:00 a.m. to 8:30 p.m. Catch the 8:00 a.m. bus. In Morelia, buses leave every half-hour for Pátzcuaro. You'll catch one after lunch in Morelia.

Drivers: Leaving Guanajuato, follow signs to Irapuato on Highway 45. Just before Irapuato, take the Querétero *quota* (toll road) to the Salamanca exit, Highway 110. Get in the right lane at the toll gate. Go into Salamanca and follow the signs to Morelia (Highway 43). After lunch in Morelia, just follow the signs to Pátzcuaro. There aren't very many; good luck!

Pátzcuaro—Orientation

In contrast to sophisticated San Miguel and cosmopolitan Guanajuato, Pátzcuaro is a slow-paced Tarascan Indian town. It's also less hilly, *gracias a Dios!* (Just as you were beginning to think all Mexican towns were built on the sides of cliffs.)

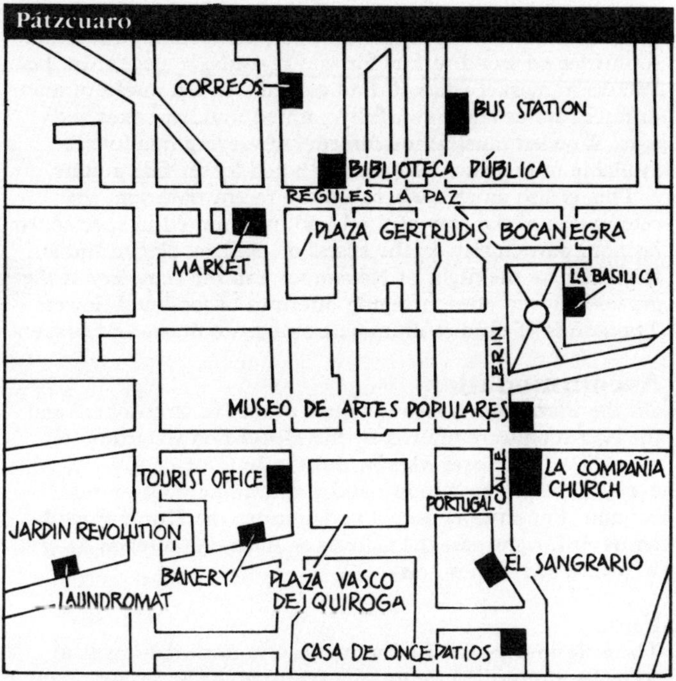

The village which grew up on the shores of this lovely lake is famous for fishermen with butterfly nets.

The origin of the Tarascan Indian culture is unknown, but the Tarascan language, Purepecha, has linguistic similarities with both the Quechua spoken by Indians in Peru and the Japanese language. Tarascan legends, customs, music and religious rites resemble those of the ancient Incas in South America. Present-day Tarascans, or Purepechans as they call themselves, are an outgoing, friendly people who have kept many of their old traditions alive.

Pátzcuaro has two main plazas: the large and formal Plaza Don Vasco and the smaller Plaza Gertrudis Bocanegra, where the 'action' is. This second plaza is the market centre to which Indians from nearby villages bring their crafts. In the sixteenth century, the Spanish bishop Don Vasco de Quiroga organised the region's villages so that each developed and perfected its own craft, preventing over-production and competition between villages. As a result, this area is rich in copperwork, wood carving, textiles, straw work and pottery. Crudely carved wooden furniture as well as more ornate and sophisticated woodwork is for sale at roadside stands. In the Pátzcuaro market you will find carved wooden masks of many different styles and colourfully painted wooden boxes and toys. Wooden musical instruments of varying quality are available in the town of Paracho, noted for its fine guitars.

This is also an area where a more recent tradition, the celebration of the Day of the Dead, is observed in spectacular fashion, particularly on the island of Janitzio. Entire Indian families pass the night of November 1 in the cemetery at the graves of loved ones, bringing offerings of food and flowers. Thousands of candles illuminate a night of music and prayers.

Accommodation

On the Plaza Don Vasco the most attractive atmosphere and the best rooms are offered by the **Hotel Los Escudos** (tel. 2-01-38). The **Hotel Mesón del Gallo** (Doctor Cos 20, tel. 2-14-74) has elegant rooms and a swimming pool—a real bargain. For cheaper accommodation try the **Hotel Posada Imperial**, right past the *Correos* at Avenida Obregon 21 (tel. 2-03-08), sometimes noisy.

Food

The hole-in-the-wall **El Portal** (across from the Basílica) specialises in grilled meats—inexpensive quick service, three kinds of homemade salsa. **El Patio** on Plaza de Don Vasco offers cheap good meals in a more elegant environment. **Los Escudos**, also on the Plaza, has moderately priced meals. **Las Redes** (The Nets) on the road to the Embarcadero has delicious budget meals and a pleasant atmosphere.

A gentle walk

Start your walk on the northern side of the Plaza Gertrudis Bocanegra de Laza de la Vega, named after a heroine of the war for independence who was shot in front of a tree on this square. Visit the public library, also named after her. After the library, turn left into Regules la Paz and walk uphill to the Basílica. Turning left out of the Basílica, walk a short way to the Museo de Artes Populares at the corner on the left. Across the street is the Iglesia de la Compañía. Continue along Calle Lerin to the Casa de Once Patios. Then retrace your steps to El Sagrario.

Turn down Calle Portugal to the Plaza de Don Vasco de Quiroga, the spacious central plaza of the town.

Sightseeing highlights

●●●**Biblioteca Pública**—The former church of San Augustin, built in the 16th century, is now the public library. The huge mural by Juan O'Gorman depicts just about everything that has happened in this area in the last 400 years. Located in Plaza Gertrudis Bocanegra. Open Mon.-Sat. 9:00 a.m.-7:00 p.m., Sun. 10:00 a.m.-1:00 p.m. and 3:00 p.m.-6:30 p.m.

●●**La Basílica**—Construction was begun in 1554, but this church was not consecrated until 1883. (Sounds like one of Steve's carpentry projects, Tina says.) The image of the Virgin Mary was made by the Indians in 1540 out of corn stalk paste, a technique of this area.

●●●**Museo de Artes Populares** (Folk Art Museum)—The beautiful patio full of flowers complements the collection of fine weavings, woodwork and ceramics. See the miniature wax figures intricately clothed in Victorian styles, old *retablos* (paintings on wood attesting to miracles and healings), a feather 'painting' of a monk and his dog, and a Day of the Dead altar. In Calle Lerin. Open Tue.-Sat. 9:00 a.m.-7:00 p.m., Sun. 9:00 a.m.-3:00 p.m., closed Mondays.

●**Iglesia de la Compañía** (Company Church)—The first cathedral built in the state of Michoacán.

●●●**Casa de Once Patios** (House of 11 Patios)—Formerly a convent, this building now houses small craft shops and *talleres* (workshops) where you can watch people weaving, doing lacquerware, etc. A good place to take photos. In Calle Lerin. Open daily 10:00 a.m.-2:00 p.m. and 4:00 p.m.-7:00 p.m.

●●**El Sagrario**—Pop into this old church to see its carved wooden pulpits, wooden parquet floor and golden stained-glass window that looks like a sun. In Calle Lerin.

●●●**Plaza de Don Vasco de Quiroga**—The main plaza is shaded by huge ash trees and surrounded by the portals of old colonial buildings now housing hotels, restaurants and the Tourist Information Office. A statue of Don Vasco marks the centre of the plaza.

TOUR 7

PÁTZCUARO—JANITZIO—MEXICO CITY

Today, by intricate and clever scheduling, you will visit the Pátzcuaro market, take a boat ride on beautiful Lake Pátzcuaro to the island of Janitzio and leave for Mexico City.

Suggested schedule

8:00	Breakfast in Pátzcuaro. Pack your bags for a quick afternoon departure.
9:00	Explore the market and enjoy the Plaza.
10:00	Take boat to Isla de Janitzio.
11:30	Early lunch on the island.
12:30	Boat trip back and return to hotel (budget travellers use alternate plan).
2:10	Depart by bus for Mexico City.
9:30	Check into your Mexico City hotel, and dine at a continental hour.

Getting to the island of Janitzio

Take a taxi or catch a bus marked *Lago* in Avenida las Américas to the *Embarcadero* (pier). Colourfully painted canopied boats leave as they fill up, about one every twenty minutes. The trip to the island takes half an hour. You'll have about 1½ hours on the island.

Take the walk up to the big ugly statue of Morelos that dominates the island and view the lake and other islands. Don't miss the strange mural inside the statue. On your way up the winding cobblestoned street you'll have had a chance to review all the restaurants to select one for lunch. In picking a restaurant, a good rule of thumb is to eat where the displayed *chile rellenos* (stuffed chilis fried in batter) are the freshest and least greasy-looking. The **Restaurant Janitzio**, the last restaurant on the dock, to your left as you face the water, has very good local *pescado blanco* (whitefish) and so-called *trucha* (trout). Steve was actually served a bass. It's very Indian, with handmade tortillas and a view. For an even better view, try a restaurant up the hill.

Bring some small notes, if you don't want to work off your meal washing dishes! Restaurants often have trouble finding change, and a 20,000 peso note might as well be a £50 note.

Getting back to Mexico City

Drivers can take the *Ruta Corta* (short route) to Mexico City via Morelia. In Morelia, follow the signs for Moravátio, then on to Atlacomulco, Toluca and the Mexico City airport to drop off your car.

Those of you travelling by public transport will take the first-class Tres Estrellas de Oro bus from Pátzcuaro at 2:10 p.m. arriving in Mexico City at 9:00 p.m.

In-tour extensions

If you have extra time, we recommend making a base in Pátzcuaro and taking day trips to nearby villages.

Santa Clara del Cobre produces the beautiful copperwork you've seen in the Pátzcuaro market. You won't necessarily find better deals in the village, but you'll definitely see a wider selection. Start with the Museo del Cobre (Copper Museum) on the left side of the street just before the main square, open daily 9:00 a.m.-7:00 p.m. There you will get an idea of the quality of work that is available if you take the time to look around. Walk around and visit the many shops. To see artisans at work, try the Casa Grande, a short way past the museum on the road to Pátzcuaro. Walk through the shop and straight to the back. Someone there will explain the process, in Spanish, if you ask. Santa Clara is about a 25-minute drive from Pátzcuaro, or you can catch a local bus.

Tzintzuntzan: This onomatopoetic Tarascan word means 'Place of the Hummingbird'. The village was once the capital of the province. Its central industry is the production of fanciful straw work. To get there, take the bus marked *Quiroga* from Pátzcuaro. On the right just before you get to town are the ruins of a pre-Hispanic city that was the centre of an empire including the entire state of Michoacán. There's a great view of the lake from the ruins.

Train trip

If you are following our itinerary but have time to travel at a more leisurely pace, you may enjoy the overnight train ride to Mexico City, leaving Pátzcuaro at 9:41 p.m. and arriving at 8:00 a.m. We took an *alcoba*, a really comfortable sleeper, which cost next to nothing. Buy your tickets at the train station at 4:00 p.m. If you are travelling on a weekend, get them a couple of days ahead.

TOUR 8

MEXICO CITY—OAXACA

Today you'll take one giant step (by air) from central to southern Mexico. You'll immerse yourself in one of the most colourful market-places in all of Mexico and visit two fascinating museums displaying pre-Columbian treasure and artefacts. Round off your day watching a performance of regional folk dancing.

Suggested schedule

6:00	Check in at Mexico City Airport.
6:30	Flight to Oaxaca. Upon arriving, make your reservations for Day 15 on Aeromexico flight 513 from Villahermosa to Mérida.
7:30	Take taxi or hired car to hotel and settle in. Have breakfast and, if you're going to tour the outlying villages tomorrow, make your arrangements now (see 'Transport', Tour 9).
10:00	To *tianguis*, the giant Saturday market. Prepare to be overwhelmed!
2:00	Back to town for lunch and a snooze.
4:00	Walking tour.
6:30	Dinner and bed, or see the folk dancers at Hotel Monte Albán.

Oaxaca Airport orientation

When you arrive, before you do anything else, buy a taxi ticket at the counter with the sign *Boletos* (Tickets), near the luggage claim area. The only transport into town is by *colectivo*, which will drop you at your hotel.

The airport Tourist Information Office will give you a package with a map of the city, information about the ruins in French, Spanish and butchered English, a list of hotels and a calendar in Spanish of the current cultural events.

If you want to hire a car, there are several companies at the airport and one in town.

Oaxaca

Twenty years ago, when we first saw the purple blossoms of the jacaranda trees against the deep blue of the sky, we fell in love with Oaxaca and its valley. Nature's dramatic setting for the city is a broad fertile plain surrounded on all sides by mountains. Equally dramatic and colourful are the Indians of the more than seventy tribes in the state, many of whom continue to dress in their distinctive *traje* (traditional Indian dress). This beautiful clothing is a feast for the eyes in the market-place, on the backs of ordinary people rather than in a museum. Oaxaca's exciting market is one of the best places in Mexico to shop for clothing, rugs and blankets and such unusual items as carved gourd rattles and bamboo drums, all made by Zapotec and Mixtec Indians.

The hub of life is the *zócalo*. Oaxaca's large and stately public garden, with its white latticework bandstand and surrounding pavement cafés, is a centre of bustling activity all day and late into the night. Oaxaca is also politically active, and the last few times we've been there thousands of teachers paraded around the *zócalo*, bearing banners and chanting '*País petrolero, pueblo sin dinero!*' ('A country with oil, the people without money!')

Oaxaca (from an Aztec word meaning 'place of the gourds') was founded in 1532. Altitude: 5,000 ft. Population: 240,000.

Accommodation

The best place to stay in town is the **El Presidente** (Calle 5 de Mayo 300, tel. 6-06-11). Located in the ex-Convent of Santa Catalina, this is one of the most beautiful hotels in Mexico, but it is well above our price range for de luxe hotels. Even if you're not staying there, it's worth visiting for buffet breakfast or a drink. Also very nice are the **Marqués del Valle** on the *zócalo* (tel. 6-31-98) and the **Monte Albán** (Calle de Leon 1, tel. 6-37-77).

A good moderately priced hotel is the **Plaza** (Trujano 112, tel. 6-40-20). We also like the **Hotel Antiquera** (Av. Hidalgo 807, tel. 6-40-20). Not as central, the **Mesón del Angel** (Mina 518, tel. 6-66-66) boasts a large swimming pool.

Our favourite budget hotel is the **Del Valle** (Diáz Ordaz 205; be careful not to confuse it with another hotel of the same name on Aldama). Get a second floor room; there's a nice terrace. The **Posada Margarita** (Plaza Labastida 115) is another good budget choice.

Food

Oaxaca isn't one of our favourite eating towns, but it offers a distinctive regional cuisine. This is the land of black beans and huge corn tortillas called *blanditas* ('little softies', though they're neither little nor particularly soft). Oaxaca is famous for its many varieties of *mole* sauce—some are *picante* (hot), nearly all are flavourful. The *fondas* (market restaurants) in the central market are a good place for the adventurous to try out some regional specialities. Be sure to ask the price first. There are no menus and *fondas* sometimes overcharge tourists.

Our best meal in Oaxaca was at the expensive **Restaurant Ajos y Cebollas** (Garlic and Onions), Calle de la Aldama 605 across from Juárez Park. They serve excellent meats, pastas and seafood. There is a bar and live music at night. Try the *filete Tampiqueña* if you are a steak eater. Another of our favourites, at cheaper prices, is the **Restaurant Santa Fe** at 103 Cinco de Mayo up from Hidalgo. The **Restaurant Catedral**, not far from the *zócalo* on the corner of Morelos and Garcia Vigil, is clean and pleasant with decent food and fast service. Vegetarians will want to try **El Arco de Emmanuel** on Calzada Chapultepec 1023. They also have a health food store. Vegetarian friends have also recommended **Pisces Restaurant** (Hidalgo 119)—*comida corrida* only.

Try the **D'Artagnan** (Hidalgo 1011) for an international menu, moderately expensive.

One of our favourite Oaxacan restaurants is the **Coronita** in the Hotel del Valle (Diáz Ordaz 208, off Hidalgo), featuring well-prepared regional cuisine at quite moderate prices; the afternoon *comida corrida* is excellent. You'll also find good, moderately priced traditional Oaxacan food in a slightly off-beat but pretty colonial patio at Restaurant **Típico de Oaxaca** (Calle Antonia Labastida 118, near Hotel Presidente). The **Restaurant Colonial**, on 20 de Noviembre up from Hidalgo, serves a tasty, cheap *comida corrida* starting at 2:00 or 2:30.

For a quick tasty lunch in a Mexican version of a fast food restaurant, go to **El Mesón** in Hidalgo just off the *zócalo*. They serve Oaxacan dishes, *pozole* and *tacos*.

Quench your thirst with a fresh juice or *liquado* (smoothie) at **Jugos La Tropical** on the corner of Garcia and Mina near the Mercado de Artesanías. Very clean. Desserts, too.

Several popular tourist restaurants in the *portales* around the *zócalo* tend to be expensive with slow service, but they're good for people-watching. You can order a beer or soft drink, enjoy the atmosphere and save your eating for better places.

Oaxaca walking tour

Leaving the cathedral, walk up Macedonia Alcalá, which is pleasantly blocked off from traffic, to the astounding Templo de Santo Domingo de Guzman. Visit the Regional Museum next door. Continue up Macedonio Alcalá and turn left,

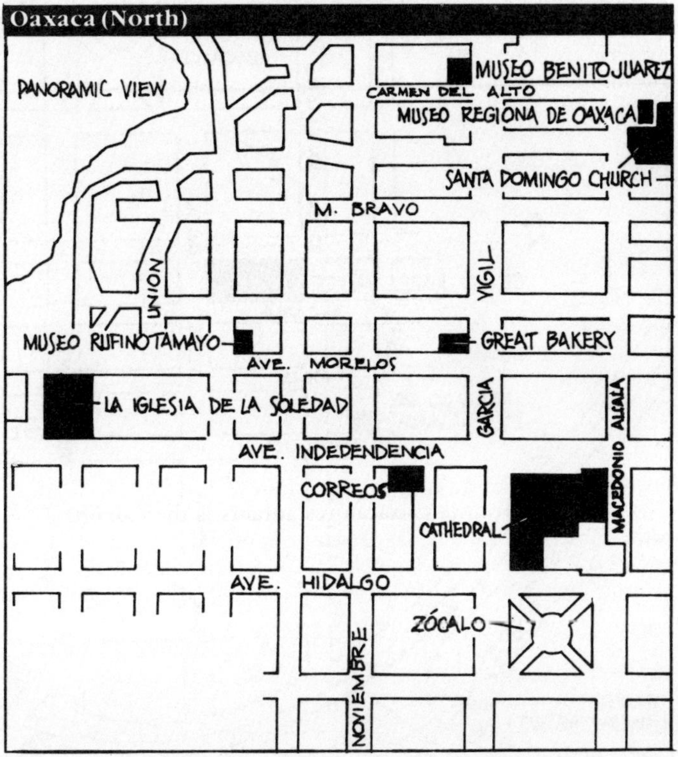

walking through the Plazuela del Carmen del Alto. Turn right at the next corner and go a short way up the street to the Benito Juárez Museum on the left. Turn back down Vigil to Avenida Morelos, then turn right and visit the Museo de Arte Prehispánico de México Rufino Tamayo. Continue in the same direction along Morelos, and just after Unión turn left into the complex of La Iglesia de la Soledad.

Sightseeing highlights

●**La Catedral**—Located next to the *zócalo*, this massive cathedral was begun in 1553 but was damaged several times by earthquakes and rebuilt in a variety of styles. On the main altar is a bronze statue of the Virgin by the Italian sculptor Tadolini.

●●●**Museo Regional de Oaxaca**—This fascinating museum, housed in a beautiful former convent adjoining

Oaxaca (South)

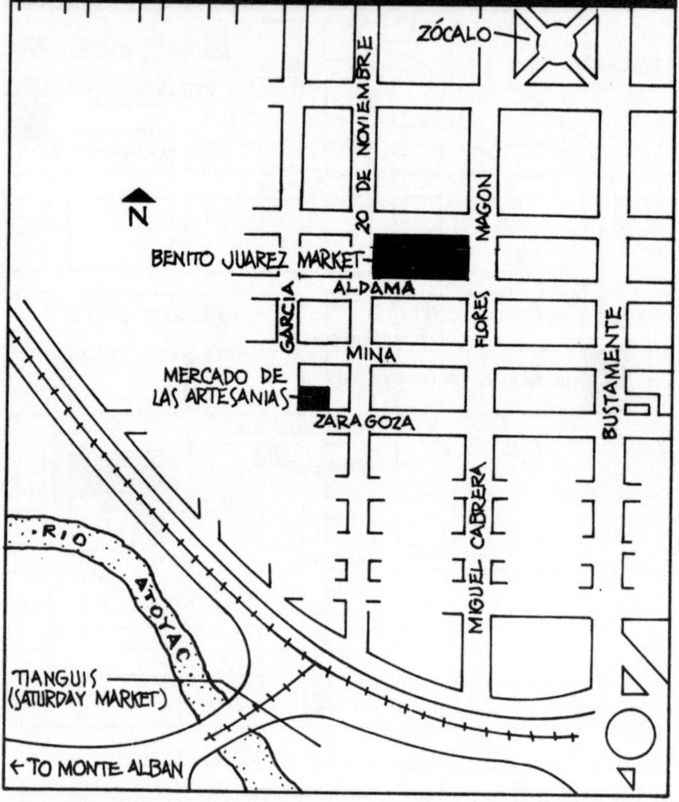

Santo Domingo church, has sections devoted to fine old examples of regional dress, ancient ceramics and gorgeous jewellery from Monte Albán's Tomb 7 (false fingernails made of gold). Skulls dating to the third epoch give evidence that this sophisticated culture experimented with brain surgery. Open Tue.-Fri. 10:00 a.m.-6:00 p.m., Sat. and Sun. 10:00 a.m.-7:00 p.m.

●●●**Templo de Santo Domingo** (Santo Domingo Church)—Begun in 1551 by Dominican friars with only 2½ pesos in their treasury, it was finally finished in 1666. The baroque gilded decoration of the interior defies description. The arched ceiling of the entrance is covered by what appears to be an elegant depiction of the Tree of Life. It is, in fact, the family tree of Don Felix de Guzman, father of the Dominicans' founder. Designated a National Monument in 1976, this church is one of the most important architectural works in the Americas. Even if churches bore you, don't miss it.

●●**Museo Benito Juárez**—Juárez, often called the Abraham Lincoln of Mexico, was a Zapotec Indian who became president of Mexico when the French were driven out in the 1860s. He instituted many liberal reforms, in addition to ordering the execution of the Emperor Maximilian by firing squad. Juárez lived in this simple house for twelve years when he first moved to Oaxaca from his native village. Open Tue.-Sun. 10:00 a.m.-2:30 p.m. and 3:30-7:00 p.m.

●●●**Museo de Arte Prehispánico de México Rufino Tamayo**—The famous Oaxacan painter Rufino Tamayo collected these pre-Columbian artefacts over a twenty-year period and donated them to the people of Oaxaca—an exquisite museum. Open 10:00 a.m.-2:00 p.m. and 4:00 p.m.-7:00 p.m., closed Tuesdays.

●●**La Iglesia de la Soledad** (Church of Solitude)—Legend has it that this old church was founded on the spot where a mule carrying a big load lay down and refused to move. The muleteer opened the cargo and discovered an image of the Virgin. The mule was dead. The Virgin is displayed in the church. See the 2-kilo gold crown decorated with 600 diamonds!

Oaxaca Saturday market (tianguis)

Until recently the *tianguis* was held in the streets of the town. Though it lost a little flavour when it moved to modern quarters on the edge of town, it's much easier to find your way around and still rates as one of the most interesting and largest Indian markets in all of Latin America. You'll find arts and crafts from throughout the region on sale. If you're interested in buying a rug or blanket, wait until you visit Teotitlán del Valle where they are made.

For further local information, you can consult the Tourist Office at the corner of 5 de Mayo and Morelos. For more information on shopping, see *The Shopper's Guide to Mexico*, (John Muir Publications, 1989, available from Horizon Books), chapter 9.

TOUR 9

TLACOLULA AND RUINS

Today's action-packed schedule will take you to an Indian market at an outlying village, several important and striking Zapotec ruins, and a town famous for its woven rugs and blankets. Finish up with a visit to one of the largest and oldest trees in the Americas.

Suggested schedule

9:00	Take the transport of your choice to Sunday market in Tlacolula.
11:30	Mitla. See the ruins and shop. Visit the museum.
1:30	Lunch at Museo Frissell in the village.
2:30	Visit the ruins of Yagul.
3:30	Visit the shops and homes of rug makers in Teotitlán del Valle.
5:00	See the ruins of Dainzú and the Tule Tree on your way back to Oaxaca.
6:00	Dinner and join the Sunday evening promenade on the *zócalo*.

Transport

You can do the trip by bus, but we don't recommend it because you'll be visiting so many places. Instead, hire a car or taxi for the day or take a guided tour from a travel agency in Hotel Presidente, Hotel Marqués del Valle or Hotel Señorial. Check a day ahead, as you may need reservations. Drivers, follow the signs on Highway 190.

Sightseeing highlights

●●●**Mitla**—This Zapotec archaeological site was occupied as early as 100 A.D. Later, when Monte Albán was abandoned, Mitla became the valley's most important centre. The ruins feature elaborate geometric ornamentation. There are two main groups: the Church Group and the Column Group. The name 'Mitla' comes from a Náhuatl word meaning 'Place of the Dead'. Open daily 8:00 a.m.-6:00 p.m.

●●●**Museo Frissell**—Located in central Mitla near the small plaza, this museum has a very good collection of local artefacts. Open daily 9:00 a.m.-6:00 p.m. The museum restaurant serves lunch at 1:30 p.m.

Much of the clothing sold in Oaxaca city comes from Mitla. You can get a slightly better price here, but you have to work at it. There's a market near the ruins and lots of shops in the village.

●●**Yagul**—1,400-year-old ruins on a hillside command a beautiful view of the valley. There are three tombs and a big stone frog representing the rain god. Open daily 9:00 a.m.-6:00 p.m.

●●●**Teotitlán del Valle**—This Zapotec Indian village is world famous for its weavings. Influenced by innovative buyers' requests, craftspeople have been weaving reproductions of works by such painters as Escher and Picasso as well as continuing to produce their own beautiful designs. If you want 100% wool, examine your choice in the sunlight and look for the tell-tale shine of acrylic. Many weavers use a blend.

●**Dainzú**—This large ruin is only partially reconstructed. Interesting rock carvings.

●●**The Tule Tree**—Located in the village of Santa Maria del Tule on Highway 190 a few miles outside of the city, this awesome tree deserves a visit. The circumference of this magnificent 2,000-year-old tree is greater than its 125-foot height.

TOUR 10

MONTE ALBÁN

After a late breakfast and an easy morning poking around markets, you'll spend the afternoon in the Zapotec ruin of Monte Albán, overlooking the valley of Oaxaca. Let your children, or the child inside you, play in the tunnels and hidden passageways.

Suggested schedule

9:00	After a leisurely breakfast (such as the buffet at Hotel Presidente) spend the morning shopping in the Benito Juárez Market and at the nearby Mercado de Artesanías.
12:00	Lunch in town. If you aren't hungry, pick up some snacks to take along as there are only soft drinks at the ruins.
12:30	Leave for Monte Albán. Allow at least 3 hours to see these ruins.
6:00	Dinner in town. You might want to pick up some fruit for tomorrow's breakfast and early departure. You can also buy your bus tickets for tomorrow now.

Sightseeing highlights

●●●**Mercado Benito Juárez**—Located near the *zócalo*. This old market is an excellent place to buy local arts and crafts and handwoven clothing. You will have to bargain hard, but a fair deal for all concerned can be had. If an occasional vendor is surly or gets angry when you offer to bargain, just move on. Oaxaca is one of the few places in Mexico where you sometimes encounter unfriendly people, especially in the markets. Don't take it personally; Mexicans from other parts of the country tell us they get the same treatment. Fortunately, most Oaxacans are friendly.

●●**Mercado de Artesanías** (Arts and Crafts Market)—This market has a large selection of local *artesanía* but it tends to be more expensive than other markets. Still worth a look.

Transport

Monte Albán is a half-hour drive from Oaxaca, six miles—straight up. Hired car people, follow your map and be very careful on the curves. *Colectivos* leave for the ruins from the Hotel Mesón del Angel (Mina 518) at 9:30 a.m., 10:30 a.m., 11:30 a.m., 12:30 p.m. and 3:30 p.m. They sell return tickets and stay only 1½ hours, so if you want to stay longer you'll have to buy two tickets and return on a later bus. Other alternatives are to hire a taxi or go on a guided tour, offered by several travel agencies in town. Check at the Hotel Presidente, Hotel Marqués del Valle or Hotel Señorial for information.

Monte Albán

On a mountaintop overlooking the entire Oaxaca Valley, Monte Albán is one of Mexico's most impressive ruins. The site was occupied for over 1,200 years, from 500 B.C. to 750 A.D. when most of the inhabitants apparently abandoned them. The Zapotecs who built these temples and ceremonial centre are the ancestors of the valley's present-day Indian population, many of whom still speak the ancient Zapotec language. Be sure to see Tomb 104 with its beautifully preserved wall paintings. If it's closed when you get to it, try again later.

The ruins and adjoining museum are open daily from 8:00 a.m. to 5:00 p.m. Guide service is available at the museum in English, French or Spanish for a minimal fee. Buy a guidebook in English at the museum shop if you don't hire a guide. The museum also has a tourist information booth.

Hint: Wear casual clothes and walking shoes, and bring a torch if you like poking around in tunnels and underground passages.

Walk through the Ruins

After buying your ticket at the museum, walk up the road to the main entrance. On your left as you enter the **Great Plaza** is the **Ball Court**. This court lacks the stone hoops or rings of the later Toltec game courts. The steps on either side of the court probably served to hold the stucco facing in place. Continuing along the eastern side of the plaza you will find platforms that served as housing and two temples. The first of these pyramids has an interior stairway to the top as well as an underground tunnel linking it to the central buildings.

The three linked **Central Buildings** contain an altar where the famous jade bat mask was found. The fourth central building, called **Mound J**, is arrow-shaped and decorated with

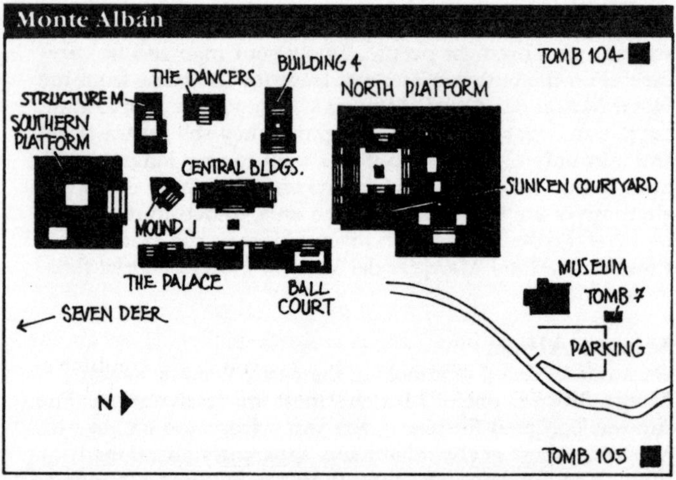

sculptural glyphs. At the southern end of the plaza, appropriately enough, you'll find the **Southern Platform**, one for true climbers. The hike to the top provides a remarkable view of the Plaza and surrounding countryside, including the complex of buildings to the south-east called **Seven Deer**, named after the glyph on its lintel. Continue clockwise to the buildings on the western side of the plaza. The first, **Structure M**, has a central stairway topped by four pillars. The next building is **Los Danzantes**, the famed building of the Dancers, named after the series of slabs carved with human figures in various attitudes. Many of these figures have strongly negroid features and are cited by some to support the theory of an ancient seeding of Mexico by the Phoenicians of Africa. On the north-west end of the plaza is **Building 4**, with an altar in the central patio and a tunnel excavated to reveal an earlier building. The stairway of the **Northern Platform** has a sanctuary on either side; the eastern one has a number of reliefs and **Stele 9**, sculpted on four sides. At the top of the stairway are two rows of columns and the Sunken Courtyard with its altar. A path to the north-west leads you to **Tomb 104**; all four of its interior walls are covered with murals. On your walk back east to the museum and car park you will come to **Tomb 7**, where the treasures exhibited in the Oaxaca Museum were found. East of the road that leads to Monte Albán is **Tomb 105**, also famous for its interior murals. The trick to visiting these tombs is finding out when they are *really* open.

In-tour extensions

If you love Oaxaca like we love Oaxaca, you won't want to tear yourself away after a mere two days. There's enough to keep you here for at least a week.

Check the market list at the back of this book. You can enjoy an Indian market any day of the week in or near Oaxaca City; some days have two or three to choose from.

San Bartolo Coyotepec is worth a visit any day of the week. Visit the *alfarería* (pottery studio) of the famous Doña Rosa, who died in 1981. Her son Valente Nieto Real continues making pottery and does pottery demonstrations on request. The courtyard has shelves of pottery for sale and a gallery of framed photographs and newspaper articles about Doña Rosa on the wall. (On a Friday, you could combine a trip to San Bartolo Coyotepec with a trip to the market at **Ocotlán de Morelos**).

Puerto Escondido is just a hop, skip and jump by air from the valley of Oaxaca. Once a tiny fishing village, it is now a popular tourist spot, with sports fishing and tours available by boat and on horseback. This is a handy place to fit in a few extra days on the beach. There are two flights daily from Oaxaca City on Oaxaca-Aerovias Oaxaqueños airlines. Their office is near the *zócalo* in Oaxaca at Armente y Lopez 209.

Accommodation: One of the more elegant hotels in Puerto Escondido is the **Hotel Santa Fe**, Calle del Morro (tel. 2-01-70), overlooking the sea at the south-eastern tip of the bay. It has a swimming pool, craft and clothing shop and a nice restaurant. The best value in town is the **Hotel Rincon del Pacifico**, centrally located on the main street at Avenida Perez Gasga 900 (tel. 2-00-56). Big airy rooms surround a courtyard of palm trees, and its restaurant is one of the best in town. Steve's friend Señor Cortez, the local pharmacist, recommends the *huachinango al horno* (baked red snapper). On the same street, up the hill, are the moderately priced **Hotel Loren** and the **Hotel Nayer**. The **Hotel Villa Marinero** on the beach (tel. 2-01-80) has *cabañas* that sleep up to four, with kitchens. If you're a frustrated cook, tired of too much restaurant eating, this is a good place to stay home for breakfast.

Restaurants: We recommend the **Restaurant Hipocampo**. Steve also likes the **Il Cappuccino** for breakfast—great fruit salads.

What to do: Go to the beach. You needn't bring along a mid-morning snack: just as hunger starts to strike, a beach vendor is likely to pop up selling bags of peanuts, *gelatinas* (jelly cups), sweet *tamales* or corn-on-the-cob. In fact, you can spend your entire day looking at jewellery, hammocks and even clothing. Of course, this can get somewhat annoying, if you're keen on gazing and daydreaming or reading a good novel instead of shopping.

There are more secluded beaches in the area. You can walk to Playa Zicatela, the next beach south, and get away from some of the madness. There are also tours to various beaches and *lagunas*; check with Turismo Manacar, at Av. Perez Gasga 302, or FCQ's Travel Service on the corner of Av. Perez Gasga and Andador Libertad.

A word to the wise: Women should not walk alone on the beach here at night. There is also petty thievery, even during the day.

TOUR 11

OAXACA—SAN CRISTÓBAL

Today will be a 'hard travelling' day. Most of your time and energy will be spent getting from Oaxaca to San Cristóbal de las Casas, where you'll enter the world of the highland Mayas.

Suggested schedule

7:00	Early bird departure on Omnibus Cristóbal Colón to San Cristóbal de las Casas leaving from the Terminal Central de Autobuses on Calzada Heroes de Chapultepec.
6:00	Arrive San Cristóbal, check into hotel, dine and rest (in order of preference).

San Cristóbal de las Casas

Altitude 6,800 feet, population 40,000. This highland Mayan town is only 87 miles from the Guatemalan frontier, and its cultural connections with the neighbouring country are evident to anyone who has travelled farther south. You will find Indians tenaciously maintaining their traditions. The state of Chiapas is one of the few remaining areas in Mexico where Indian *men* continue to dress in traditional village *traje*. They look impressive. It's hard to believe that men dressed in bright pink ponchos, trousers like white pedal-pushers and straw hats festooned with ribbon streamers could maintain their dignity, but they certainly do. The highland Mayan Indians sell traditional clothing, woollen ponchos and nice leatherwork. Some of Mexico's finest textile work is done in the San Cristóbal area. You will also find Guatemalan weavings.

The beautiful mountainous countryside is highly cultivated. Little *milpas* (cornfields) crisscross the outrageously steep slopes, often causing Steve to exclaim, 'Aren't you glad you don't have to water *that*!' To the Indians, a piece of earth, however small and inaccessible, is precious and to be cultivated with care. Many of them derive their only livelihood selling small crops of corn or vegetables from these plots.

The town of San Cristóbal was founded in 1528. Each of its several *barrios* (districts) spoke a different language and had its own church. Each *barrio* tended to have its own speciality, such as breeding pigs, weaving, firework-making or masonry. What is now the market area formerly specialised in sweets. There were the toymakers of Guadalupe, the potters of San Ramón, the woodcutters, charcoal makers and launderers of Santa Lupe. Some deep-rooted traditions persist, but today the mule drivers of San Diego deliver merchandise to nearby villages by truck.

Accommodation

The **Santa Clara**, on the corner of the plaza (Av. Insurgentes 1, tel. 8-11-40), is the sixteenth-century former home of Diego de Mazariezgo. The hotel has a lot of charm, with colourful red macaws on the patio. The warmest rooms are on the second floor.

Almost next door, the **Hotel de Ciudad Real** (Plaza 31 de Mayo 10, tel. 8-01-87) is just as nice and better value. It has a very pretty roofed courtyard restaurant with flowers, ferns and a small parrot. The most expensive hotel in town is not as nice as the **Hotel Español** (Iro de Marzo 16, tel. 8-00-45), which has big rooms with fireplaces, a feature you may want to take advantage of in this town. Also in the moderate price range are **Hotel Palacio de Moctezuma** (Av. Juárez 16, tel. 8-03-52) and the **Hotel Fray Bartolome de las Casas** (Niños Héroes 2, tel. 8-09-32). The best budget accommodation is found at the **Casa Margarita** (Calle Real de Guadalupe 34). Or try the **Hotel San Martín**, just east of the *jardín* (Calle Real de Guadalupe 16, tel. 8-05-33). Other budget accommodation is to be found at **Pension Ramos** (Calle Cuahtemoc 12).

Food

For an elegant dining room overlooking the *zócalo*, try the restaurant **La Plaza**, whose entrance is at Hidalgo 1. The *comida corrida* is expensive for San Cristóbal, but the entrées are quite reasonable and very good. **El Unicorno** at 35 Insurgentes specialises in steaks, pizza and delicious soups. For atmosphere, you can't beat **El Fogon de Tovel**, 11-16 de Septiembre, where waiters dressed in traditional *traje* serve you on a charming patio while a marimba band plays softly.

Another favourite of ours is the restaurant of the **Hotel Palacio de Moctezuma** (Av. Juárez 7)—very pretty courtyard, good food, moderate prices, what more could you ask for? The restaurant **El Mesón Coleto** in Madero a short way from the *zócalo* has a good *comida corrida* between 1:00 and 5:00 p.m.

Restaurant Lacanja, 130A 1 de Marzo, offers very

inexpensive breakfasts and reasonably priced meals. For a quick breakfast or lunch, try **Los Arcos** just off the *zócalo* in Madero. The 'in' coffeehouse in town is **La Galería**, Hidalgo 3, with a gallery/boutique downstairs, coffee upstairs. You can also get a good cup of coffee in the gazebo in the centre of the plaza, open until 11:00 p.m., or at **La Troje**, near the *correos*.

Helpful hints

The Tourist Office on the north-west corner of the plaza has lots of photo displays, maps and information on nearby villages. They also have the record player that plays piped music on the plaza. Have a look at their records and see if there's a favourite you'd like them to play.

Shopping: Look for leatherwork, handsome and simple woollen ponchos, primitive dolls and Guatemalan crafts. We like to buy dolls and the simpler woollen weavings from the women on the street and in the plaza in front of Santo Domingo church. In the main square, you will find yourself surrounded by Indian ladies waving woven bracelets and anklets in your face.

For more details on the beautiful weavings and other handicrafts available in this area, see *The Shopper's Guide to Mexico*, chapter 10.

At the **Baños Mercedarios**, 1 de Marzo and 12 de Octubre, you can hire a private room and luxuriate in a steam bath, often a welcome warmer-upper in this climate.

TOUR 12

SAN CRISTÓBAL DE LAS CASAS

Today you'll explore San Cristóbal, admire (and perhaps buy) the textiles of an Indian weaving cooperative and visit the home of the famous archaeologists Frans Blom and Gertrude Duby.

Suggested schedule

9:00	Breakfast.
10:00	Walking tour.
2:00	Lunch and free time for shopping.
4:00	Taxi to Casa Na-Bolom and take tour.
5:30	Get bus tickets to Palenque for tomorrow morning at 8:30 a.m. If you are planning a side trip to Bonampak and Yaxchilán (see 'In-Tour Extensions' Tour 14), phone ahead for reservations.
6:00	Dinner.

Walking tour

Starting at the Cathedral, notable for its carved wooden ceilings and the birds living in it, take Calle Utrilla towards the market, visiting shops on the way. Explore the market and pick up some snacks for tomorrow's trip. Now retrace your steps down Calle Utrilla and turn right along Comitán, into the complex of the Templo y Convento de Santo Domingo. Next door to the church is the weavers' cooperative of Santa Jolobil. Return to the plaza and walk up Calle Real de Guadalupe, enjoying poking in all the shops, to the beautiful blue and white Templo de Guadalupe. Enjoy the 360-degree view and bring your heart rate back down to normal. Returning to the plaza, you might want to explore the shops in Calle Real de Guadalupe.

Bus tickets

The bus station is in Ignacio Allende on the Periférico (ring road). The first-class bus service is the Tuxtla. The trip to Palenque takes about 6 hours.

San Cristóbal

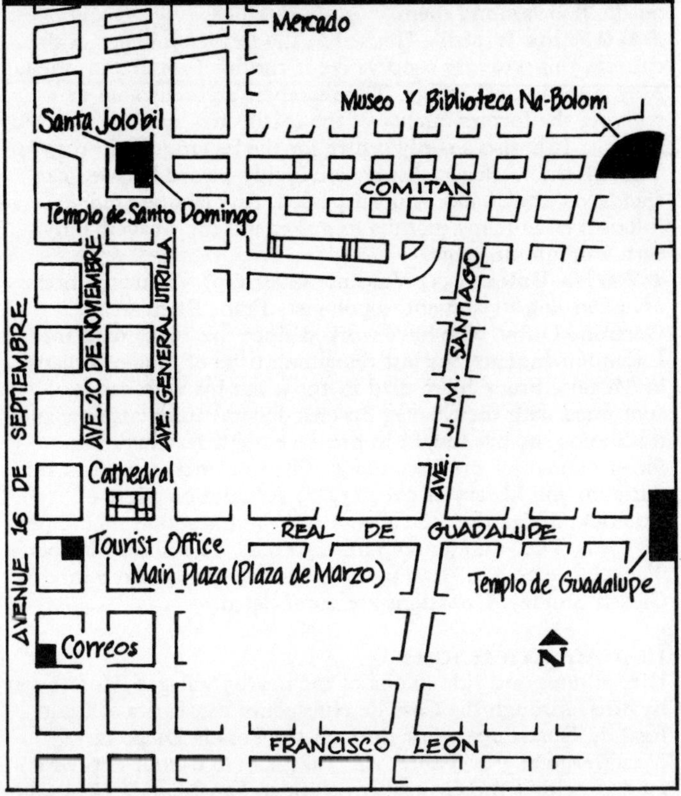

Sightseeing highlights

●**Cathedral**—Don't miss the ornate baroque altarpiece.

●●●**Mercado**—Watch Indians from the various villages congregate to sell their wares, do their shopping and exchange news. If you need an excuse to stand around and stare, buy an *elote* (corn on a stick, with or without chile and lime) or a bag of peanuts to munch.

●●●**Templo de Santo Domingo**—The walls and pulpit of this sixteenth-century church are encrusted with gold. There is a smell of copal incense, a tree resin used by the Indians as an offering since ancient times. The floral decorations are elaborate and lovely. If you're lucky, you may happen upon an Indian *curandero* (healer) doing a *limpia* (cleansing) on a client. We watched a *curandero* here use eggs for the cleansing, chanting prayers with many candles burning on the floor around them.

●●●**Santa Jolobil**—Housed in the former convent of the church, this weaving cooperative is run by Tzotzil and Tzeltal Mayan traditional artists. The members are dedicated to reviving the former quality of the textile arts and use very old designs. It is also a study centre for the technique of brocade. Though the works on display are highly-priced by Mexican standards, the quality is unsurpassed. An elaborate *huipil* (blouse) takes many months to make, and the weavers only earn a minimum wage.

●●●**Na-Bolom** (333 Vincente Guerrero)—Tour the home of archaeologists and anthropologists Frans Blom and Gertrude Duby, who have worked since the 1950s with the Lacandón Indians, the last remaining tribe of jungle Indians in Mexico. Frans Blom died in 1963, but his wife has continued with their work. Besides documenting customs and traditions, she has fought to preserve the threatened rain forest domain of the Lacandóns. The tour includes the small museum and library of over 13,000 volumes on Meso-America, the garden, the chapel and the Lacandón *sala*. Open for tours Tue.-Sun., 4:00 p.m.-5:30 p.m. The library is open Tue.-Sat. 9:00 a.m.-1:30 p.m., Mon. 2:30 p.m.-6:00 p.m. Closed Sunday. Donations are appreciated.

In-tour extensions

Hire a horse and ride to one of the nearby villages. Horses can be hired through the Casa de Huespedes Margarita at Calle Real de Guadalupe 34 or through the Posada Diego de Mazariezgo at 5 de Febrero 1. Take a 4- to 6-hour trip with a guide to either the Grutas (caves) or to San Juan de Chamula. It's best to make arrangements a day in advance.

The Posada Diego de Mazariezgo travel agency also offers tours by VW bus to San Juan de Chamula, Zinacantán and the Grutas or to the Lagos de Montebello (Lakes of the Pretty Mountain). These 8-hour tours are for a minimum of 4 persons.

Combis leave from the market area in San Cristóbal all the time for nearby villages; just find the minibus marked with the name of the town you want to explore and hop aboard for a real Indian adventure.

A word to the wise: The Indians of San Juan de Chamula do not like to be photographed. Like many Indians, they believe that the camera captures their soul. It is illegal to take photographs, *strictly enforced!*

TOUR 13

SAN CRISTÓBAL—PALENQUE

After travelling from highland San Cristóbal to Palenque in the jungle lowlands of Chiapas, you'll relax in a pool and adjust to the sudden descent and tropical climate. You may have the good fortune to glimpse Lacandón Indians, the last tribal inhabitants of the Mexican rain forest, in town to shop and trade.

Suggested schedule

8:30	Bus departs for the town of Palenque. The ruins of Palenque are 5 miles out of town.
2:30	Arrive in Palenque, voracious! Check into hotel and get some lunch (or vice versa).
4:00	Cool off in the hotel swimming pool.
5:00	Make arrangements for visiting Agua Azul on Tour 15. Look around town.
6:30	Dinner.

Accommodation

When we first went to Palenque the town was a single-street village with virtually no accommodation. That has certainly changed. Now you can find a full range of hotels from the budget **Hotel Palenque** off the plaza (Av. 5 de Mayo 14) to beautiful, moderately expensive bungalows at **Hotel Chan Kah** on the road to the ruins (Km. 3). It boasts a beautiful garden with pet monkeys. We highly recommend the **Hotel Cañada** (Calle Merle Green) in town but located in a junglelike wooded area—nice bungalows quite reasonably priced but unfortunately often full. **Las Ruinas** at Km. 6 on the road to the ruins is moderately priced, with a good swimming pool that you'll really appreciate in this hot humid climate. The lowest-priced budget hotel we've found is the **Hotel La Croix** (Av. Hidalgo 18)—the beds aren't great, but there are nice murals on the walls.

Food

There are several good restaurants in and around the town of Palenque. You'll begin to notice the Yucatán Maya influence in the cooking. A very moderately priced restaurant just off the *zócalo* is the **Restaurant Maya**—clean, with a bar and Mayan specialities. Two other restaurants we like are **La Cañada** (at the Hotel Cañada mentioned before) and the nearby **Restaurant La Selva**. Both have moderate prices, bars and jungle atmosphere. On the road to the ruins the attractive **Restaurant El Paraíso** (Paradise) has moderately priced meals, a bar and marimba players. Take a taxi to this one if you're not driving a car, or catch one of the VW bus *colectivos*.

TOUR 14
PALENQUE

Palenque is among the loveliest of all Mayan ruins, and today is your chance to enjoy it. In the afternoon you'll be able to relax or do some more exploring.

Suggested schedule

8:00	Be at the ruins when they open. Explore the Temple of the Sun complex and the Palace.
9:45	Take the jungle path to the Lion Temple.
10:00	Be at the top of the Temple of the Inscriptions when they open the tomb.
10:30	Visit Northern Group, Ball Park and Museum.
12:30	Lunch.
1:00	A free afternoon to laze around your hotel pool or further explore the ruins or the little town of Palenque.
7:00	Dinner.

Palenque Ruins
The Mayan civilisation encompassed the entire Yucatán peninsula of Mexico, parts of the state of Chiapas, all of Guatemala, Belize and the north-western sections of Honduras and El Salvador. There is evidence of nomadic peoples in the area as early as 10,000 B.C, and Mayan civilisation reached its height between 300 and 900 A.D., the Classic Period. After A.D. 900 many of the great ceremonial centres mysteriously fell into disuse.

The Mayas were the only people in the Americas to develop writing, and it is only recently that the inscriptions have been deciphered. Study has revealed that most of the carved stones are historical records marking the beginnings and endings of rulers' reigns, battles, and other events.

Time and the gods were entwined concepts: each day was a god, and the rich Mayan ceremonial life centred around their calendar and the cycles of the planets. The astrologer-priests, meticulous observers of the movement of the planets, chose auspicious times to clear the forests and plant and harvest crops. The Mayan gods were the forces of nature personified—the sun, the rain, the earth and other planets.

Against the lush green jungle, the elegant tracery of the roof-combs of Palenque's Temple of the Sun and the Temple of the Inscriptions lend an almost Oriental air to the site. If you arrive early in the morning, you will have the great pleasure of experiencing the mood of the ruins and the jungle undisturbed by the noise of tourism.

There are two ways to approach a ruin. (1) The academic, armed with guidebooks, maps, binoculars and torch, comes determined to appraise, compare, collect data—in short, to research it. (2) The 'feeler' drifts through on the atmosphere of the place and absorbs ancient vibes. We've found that it's possible to blend harmoniously both types of experience by becoming knowledgeable about the site, then climbing to the top of a temple to enjoy the view and settle into quiet contemplation. In that way both the scientist and the poet in each of us is satisfied.

Getting to the Ruins

Collective taxis to the ruins leave town every 15 minutes from the office of Colectivos Chambalu, off Benito Juárez in Ignacio Allende street. Flag one down in the street, or on the main road if you're staying near the ruins. ADO bus company has a first-class bus to the ruins daily at 10:00 a.m. Taxis charge about £1.30.

Seeing the Ruins

If you're lucky, there will be Lacandón Indians at the entrance dressed in their simple white robes, selling large bows and arrows trimmed with parrot feathers. Even if you can't fit a set in your suitcase, be sure to examine their wares and give yourself the opportunity to talk with these handsome open-faced men (if only in sign language).

Walk straight in past the Temple of the Inscriptions on your right and the Palace with its tower on your left (we'll get back to these later) and cross the **Aqueduct**. On the right is the **Temple of the Sun**, which you'll climb to see the magnificent carved panel, representing the sun being worshipped by two priests, on the back wall of the shrine.

The **Temple of the Foliated Cross** faces the Temple of the Sun. The panel after which this temple was named shows a cross decorated with corn leaves and human heads. The sun god and a quetzal bird with the mask of the rain god surmount the cross. The decorative crosses at Palenque are thought to be stylised versions of the corn plant, much venerated by the early Mayas and still addressed as 'Your Grace' by Indians today. Or they may represent the ceiba

Palenque

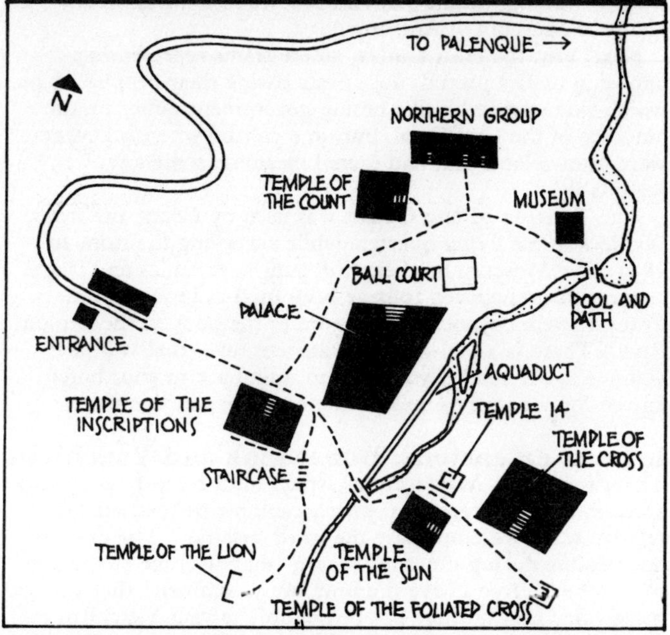

tree, the sacred tree believed to stand at the four corners of the world and at the centre of the universe.

Your third climb of the day (and you're just getting started!) will be to the top of the **Temple of the Cross**. Finish this group with **Temple 14** on your right as you head back to the Palace.

The **Palace** complex bears some exploring. Use your torch in the cellars on the southern side. The tower has an interior suitcase that starts on the first floor, which you reach from the north side.

There is a small staircase in the hillside behind the Temple of the Inscriptions. Follow it and the path to the **Temple of the Lion.** When you return, enter the top of the **Temple of the Inscriptions** from the hillside behind it, avoiding the steepest climb in the ruins. The panel to which this temple owes its name is now preserved in the National Museum of Anthropology in Mexico City. The panels on either side of the sanctuary door are well preserved. One depicts an old priest, draped in a tiger skin, smoking a cigar. The staircase and the funerary crypt were discovered in 1952. The body inside was interred under a gigantic carved slab. Also found here was a magnificent jade mask, since stolen from the National Museum of Anthropology.

Next, visit the **Ball Court**, where teams representing opposing deities played, the priests basing their prophesies on which side won (a bit like basing government policy on the outcome of the Cup Final, but, in a culture where all events were inter-related and had sacred meaning, somehow reasonable).

The **Temple of the Count** was used by Count Frederick Waldeck as his living quarters while surveying the ruins in 1833. The Museum has beautiful panels, ceramics and large clay cylinders believed to have been used as incense burners. You can walk beyond the Museum to the pool on the Otolom River. There is a path, once an ancient road, that will take you out to the road if you want to walk back to your hotel. Listen for the roar of howler monkeys away in the jungle.

In-tour extensions: Bonampak and Yaxchilán

These important Mayan ruins, which until recently were only accessible by chartered aeroplane, can now be reached with relative ease. We emphasise the word 'relative'. The drive is not feasible during the rainy season (roughly June to the end of October). If you have the time, we recommend that you see these ruins now. It may not be possible to visit Yaxchilán in the future as the Mexican and Guatemalan governments are planning a joint project to dam the Usumacinta River. Hydro-electric dams may flood many important Mayan ruins, including Yaxchilán and Piedras Negras. On top of that, the extensive Mexican rain forest is being cleared to provide grazing land. This entire magnificent jungle may soon be lost.

Getting there: A trip to either Bonampak or Yaxchilán from Palenque takes one very long day, a 9- or 10-hour round-trip over rough dirt roads. At the time of writing, the road into Bonampak had caved in, and we walked six miles in to the ruin. The walk took 4 to 5 hours. You'll want at least an hour at the ruins. The trip to Yaxchilán and back takes one-and-a-half hours in a riverboat on the Usumacinta River. We wouldn't want to spend any less than two hours at the ruins, preferably three. To visit either ruin, leave Palenque about 5:00 a.m. and return by 8:30 or 9:00 p.m.

Why visit just one of these ruins when you've made it this far? We recommend two days for this side trip, camping out overnight.

The travel agency Anfitriones Turísticos de Chiapas on the

corner of Calles Juárez and Allende in Palenque, offers a two-day trip that includes transport, camping gear and meals. The cost is £200 for up to six people, or £33 apiece on a full trip. Phone ahead from San Cristóbal to sign up for the next group (tel. 5-02-10 or 8-25-50). If your Spanish isn't good enough, ask your hotel in San Cristóbal or a travel agent to make the booking for you.

Bonampak: This compact ruin consists of one large mound, perhaps originally a single pyramid embellished with several temples and some carved stelae in the plaza. Bonampak is famous for its colourful murals depicting scenes from Mayan life. Over the years the murals were obscured by calcium deposits, and you were better off seeing the reproductions in the Museum of Anthropology in Mexico City. But the murals at Bonampak are currently being restored by fieldworkers from the Mexico City museum. Now the restored portions of the murals glow in living colour again, almost as if they had been painted yesterday. Besides the experience of the ruins themselves, you walk through the rain forest to get there. We recommend an early morning departure if possible, since it gets hot quickly in the jungle. It's a beautiful nature walk along a rutted road that deteriorates into a trail. Allow time to observe the busy work of the leafcutter ants and the myriad butterflies. You may be treated, as we were, to the sight of wild parrots in flight (remember your binoculars). You'll undoubtedly hear mysterious whirrings and thrashings off in the brush. Bring a plastic bottle of water and replenish it at the compound near the ruins.

Yaxchilán: This was a ceremonial centre during the Late Classic Period of Mayan culture (after 900 A.D.). Lacandón Indians still make pilgrimages here to make offerings and pray. It is an extensive ruin, in varying stages of restoration. Its majestic beauty is enhanced by the surrounding rain forest, and the site overlooks the broad Usumacinta River, the boundary between Mexico and Guatemala.

The locals at Frontera Corozal, the frontier town on the banks of the Usumacinta, provide transport to the ruins in their long wooden *pangas* powered by outboard motors.

TOUR 15

PALENQUE—MÉRIDA

After experiencing the magnificent waterfalls of Agua Azul, you'll travel to Villahermosa and fly from there to Mérida, the Yucatán's largest city.

Suggested schedule

7:00	Breakfast.
8:00	Tour, bus or taxi to the waterfalls of Misol-Ha and Agua Azul.
Early evening	Catch bus to Villahermosa.
8:00	Dinner in Villahermosa.
9:30	Check in at airport.
10:20	Take Aeromexico Flight 513 to Mérida.
11:15	Arrive Mérida and take taxi to hotel.

Getting to the Waterfalls

Hire a taxi to Agua Azul for about £23, and stay there up to 3 hours. Or arrange a trip with either the Cooperative de Colectivos Chambalu or the travel agency Anfitriones Turísticos de Chiapas in Calle Juárez. A trip for up to ten people is £23 and takes about 6 hours. You can take a bus as well, but you will have to walk or hitchhike the 4 km in from the highway.

Agua Azul

We've never managed to take a photograph that does Agua Azul (blue water) justice, and we challenge you to try. This is one of nature's masterpieces: a confluence of two rivers in a series of magnificent waterfalls. Follow the path along the banks of the river, swim in the large pools, loll in the little pools, or test your balance walking across one of the falls.

Mérida Airport

Before leaving the airport, make your reservations and/or buy your ticket home via Mexico City or directly to your home-town. The tourist information booth has a list of hotels and can assist you in making a reservation. The ticket office for *colectivos* and taxis is outside the front door of the airport.

Buy a ticket to avoid being overcharged. There is a large selection of car hire firms and some have special offers. There is also a *bureau de change* offering bank rates.

The Yucatán

The Yucatán Peninsula, commonly called the Yucatán, includes the states of Campeche, Yucatán and Quintana Roo. The peninsula juts northward from the southernmost part of Mexico and shares borders with Guatemala and Belize. You may feel as if you've been travelling south but, believe it or not, when you reach Isla Mujeres you are north of Mexico City, at about the same latitude as Guanajuato and only about 90 miles from Cuba.

The peninsula is as flat as the proverbial pancake. Once while travelling with our Mayan friend Nacho Bey, who had never left the Yucatán before, we were amazed when he asked if the distant mountain range ahead was some sort of huge pyramid. He'd never seen a hill! There is very little soil on the peninsula, and the limestone bedrock is evident wherever you look. The limestone is perforated with caves, and all drainage is underground, so there are no rivers or streams on the surface. The *cenotes* (natural wells) you'll see everywhere are sinkholes that formed when the roofs of limestone caves collapsed. The vegetation in the north is mostly scrub and low jungle. Most of the higher jungle has been cut for timber. The local Maya still practice ancient slash-and-burn agriculture, eking out a living to the detriment of the forest.

Though the Yucatán countryside may not have the spectacular scenery found elsewhere in Mexico, the region offers an exciting array of Mayan villages, pre-Columbian ruins, beautiful beaches and unspoiled islands.

The climate of the Yucatán is consistently hot or hotter, with the exception of *nortes*, three- or four-day north winds, usually bringing rain. On the coast, March and April are windy months.

As recently as thirty years ago the Yucatán Peninsula was all but cut off from the rest of Mexico due to lack of roads. The Mayan Indians of this region are proud of their cultural independence from the rest of Mexico. The Mayans here dress in traditional impeccable white clothing, and the dignity of their handsome faces is broken only by their broad, warm smiles and laughter.

Mérida

Mérida is a big city of half a million that feels as if it were a smaller town in a different country. It is a very Mayan city.

The Mayans are proud of their language. They are also very friendly.

Mérida was founded in 1542 by the *conquistador* Francisco Montejo. You'll see his name everywhere—from street names to a local brand of beer. Paseo de Montejo is a broad boulevard built in the 1890s, lined with mansions dating from the henequen boom. Henequen, a fibre derived from the sisal plant, is used to make rope and twine. Synthetic replacements have hurt the industry, though plantations still operate in the Yucatán countryside. It is usually hot in Mérida, so flow with the tropical rhythm of the place and do your sightseeing in the cooler morning and evening hours. Reserve the hot afternoons for siestas or pool-sitting.

Mérida's streets are numbered in a simple grid system: north-south streets are odd numbered and east-west streets are even numbered. The street numbers are sequential, with the lowest numbers on the outskirts of town. Sounds easy, but when someone says the place you're looking for is 'on the corner of Calles 58 and 59 between Calles 58 and 60', you'd have to be an international chess champion to visualise the location.

Accommodation

Mérida has lots and lots of hotels, with comfortable accommodation in all price ranges. Tina's favourite is the truly colonial **Posada Toledo** at the corner of Calles 58 and 57 (tel. 23-16-90). The dining room's ambience is elegant colonial, and the French suite is truly unusual. The **Hotel Casa de Balám** (Calle 60 488, tel. 24-88-44) is also quite charming. The **Hotel Mérida Misión** (Calle 60 491, tel. 23-95-00) is a deluxe hotel, often full.

Your best bets in the moderate range are the **Hotel Colonial** (Calle 62 476, tel. 23-64-44) or the **Hotel Caribe**, pleasantly situated at the back corner of Parque Hidalgo (tel. 24-90-22). Rooms with air conditioning cost slightly more than those with fans. The **Hotel Colón** (Calle 62 483, tel. 23-43-55) has air conditioning in all rooms.

The **Hotel Reforma** (Calle 59 508, tel. 24-79-22) is a popular budget hotel with pool (you may need a reservation). Don't take a room near the television room. We were an involuntary audience to a loud late-night boxing match. The **Hotel Mucuy** (Calle 57 481) has simple clean rooms, and the management is kind and helpful; no pool.

Food

Mérida is Steve's kind of town—lots of delicious food! The

cooking of the Yucatán is famous throughout Mexico, and justifiably so. The blending of Spanish, Mayan and Lebanese cuisines makes for some truly interesting dishes.

For traditional Mayan food, try **Restaurant Los Almendros** (Calle 50-A 493 on the Plaza Ejorada). This pleasant restaurant serves outstanding *pibil* dishes (chicken or pork cooked in a fire pit and seasoned with achiote sauce) or their speciality, *poc-chuc* (thin pieces of grilled pork with a special sauce). The **Restaurant Colón** (Calle 62 487) offers excellent regional food in a pleasant colonial patio.

For Lebanese food, **Alberto's Continental Patio** (on the corner of Calles 64 & 57) is a good choice. Located in a beautiful old colonial house and patio, they serve steaks and pastas as well as Lebanese dishes. **Cedro de Líbano,** a more moderately priced Lebanese restaurant, is located in Calle 59 between Calles 64 and 66. Our favourite 'hole-in-the-wall' Middle Eastern restaurant is **Restaurant El Arabe David** (David the Arab) at Calle 61 542. The decor is non-existent, but the food is tasty and inexpensive.

The **Restaurant Flamingos** (Calle 57 near Calle 58) is clean, has fast service and specialises in seafood and regional dishes. An attractive restaurant with patio or inside air conditioning is the **Pórtico del Peregringo** (Calle 57 501), serving seafood, international and regional dishes. For French food, go to **Restaurant Vannig** (Calle 62 480).

Restaurant Express (Calle 59 502, opposite Hidalgo Park) serves a good breakfast. Try *huevos motuleños,* a *huevos rancheros* variation.

TOUR 16

MÉRIDA

Today you'll begin your exploration of the Yucatán by foot and old-fashioned horse cab. Get acquainted with the local flora and fauna at the Mérida Zoo, then take time off for a swim (practising for your beach days).

Suggested schedule

8:00	Breakfast.
9:00	Walking tour.
10:00	Shopping in market.
11:00	Horse cab to the Museum of Anthropology.
12:00	Lunch.
1:00	Cool off in pool. (Dedicated ruins-goers—see alternative plan.)
3:00	Visit the Zoo.
6:00	Dinner.
8:00	Ballet Folklórico.

Alternative plan

Morning	Same as above, but make tour reservations instead of buying tickets to Ballet.
2:00	Take Gonzalez Agency (Calle 59 476, tel. 1-01-97) tour to Uxmal and the *son et lumière* show, returning at 11:00 p.m. £15 includes dinner.

Walking tour

Start at the Plaza Cepeda Peraza, the original plaza of Mérida (also called Parque Hidalgo). Walk down Calle 60 to Calle 59 and visit the Templo del Tercer Orden. Continuing on Calle 60, stop at the tourist office for brochures, tour information and maps. The Teatro Peón Contreras, on the next corner, usually has an art exhibition in the lobby. Buy tickets for tonight's Ballet Folklórico. Walk back along Calle 60 to the *zócalo* and visit the Cathedral. Continue south and turn left on Calle 65. At Calle 56A, turn right and a little way down you'll see a green cement stairway on the left leading up to the Mercado Municipal (city market).

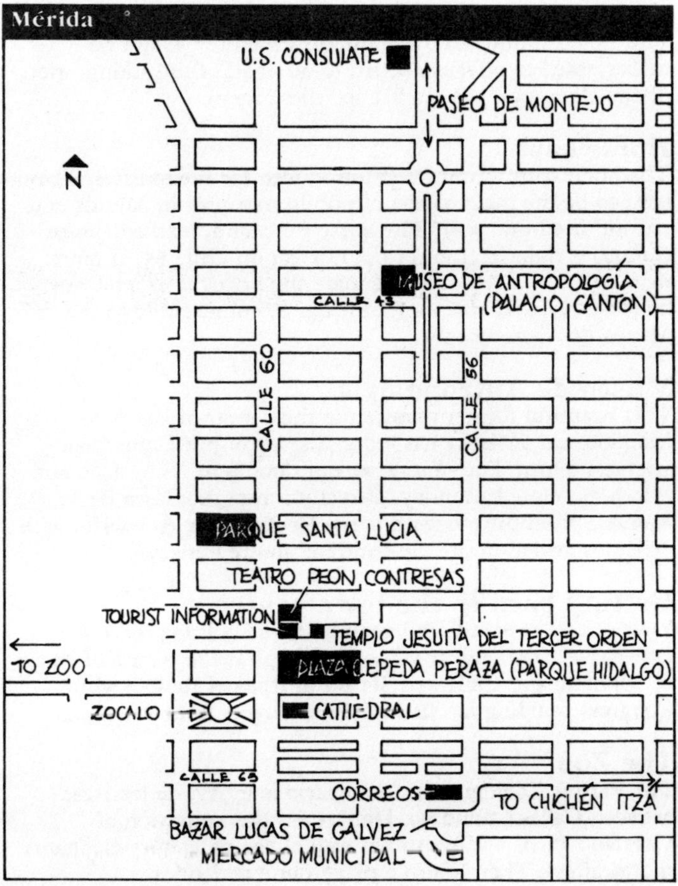

Shopping hints

Mexico's best hammocks are sold in Mérida. A word of caution: any hammock, correctly displayed, looks enormous. Many's the unhappy tourist who strings his hammock up in his garden back home, gets in and finds himself precariously balanced on a net tightrope! Buy hammocks by weight. **Cordeles Nacionales** at Calle 56 516-B gives good value. The weight of the hammock is listed in grams on the package.

Other good buys here are Panama hats, *guayaberas* and *huipiles*. The best quality Panama hats have a very fine weave and can be rolled up. *Guayaberas*, the dress shirt for work or pleasure, are worn all over Mexico. *Huipiles* are the beautiful white dresses of the Mayan women, colourfully embroidered with flowers. Shrewd bargaining is called for. Don't be embarrassed to offer one-third to one-half of the asking price. Shops all around the market sell these items.

Horse cabs

The horse cabs weren't just introduced for the tourists. They used to be the main means of public transport in Mérida and are still used that way. The horse cab stand, marked *Coches Calasa*, is right in front of the *Correos* on Calle 65. If more than one cab is available, compare the prices of several. An hour costs £4. It cost us £1 for the 20-minute ride to the Museo de Antropología

Museo de Antropología

This beautiful former mansion at the corner of Paseo de Montejo and Calle 43 has a fine display of pre-Columbian artefacts. Open Tue.-Sat. 8:00 a.m.-8:00 p.m., Sun. 8:00 a.m.-2:00 p.m., closed Monday. Directly across the Paseo de Montejo from the museum is the **Restaurant Arrecife**, with delicious grilled meats. So handy if you're hungry.

Getting back to the town centre

Your cabbie may still be hanging around waiting for a fare. Otherwise, catch any city bus that stops at the corner of Paseo de Montejo and Calle 41. Get off in front of the big white Congress building in Calle 59 a few streets from the *zócalo*.

The Zoo

The Parque Zoológico El Centenario is in Av. de los Itzaes between Calles 65 and 59. Don't miss this collection of Yucatán's birds and beasts (as well as the obligatory elephants and giraffes). There's also a playground and rides.

TOUR 17

MÉRIDA—CHICHÉN ITZÁ—ISLA MUJERES

Today you'll leave Mérida and visit the Mayan ruins of Chichén Itzá with its infamous sacred cenote, once the scene of human sacrifices. There will be time for a cooling swim before you head for Puerto Juárez and the ferry to beautiful Isla Mujeres (Island of Women).

Suggested schedule

6:30	Leave Mérida for 2-hour bus or car journey to Chichén Itzá.
8:30	Explore the ruins.
12:00	Lunch and a swim.
1:30	Leave for Puerto Juárez by bus (Drivers—see Transport: Chichén Itzá to Isla Mujeres below).
3:30	Arrive in Puerto Juárez, catch ferry to Isla Mujeres. Check into hotel.
7:00	Dinner and a walk around town.

Transport: Mérida to Chichén Itzá

The Mérida bus station, Unión de Camioneros de Yucatán, is in Calle 69 between 68 and 70. Autotransportes de Oriente has a bus leaving for Chichén Itzá at 6:30 a.m. This bus is usually full. It's best to buy your ticket the day before. Get off at the ruins, not in the village. For a small fee you can leave your luggage in a room behind the ticket office, marked *Salida*.

Chichén Itzá

Chichén Itzá gets crowded. Leave Mérida early to enjoy the ruins in the cool of the morning.

Experts believe Chichén Itzá was founded around the time of Christ. An invading people known as the Itzá (water witches or wizards) took over the city in the 4th century A.D. The name Chichén Itzá ('Well Mouth of the Water Witches') refers to the city's sacred cenote.

Some time in the 10th century A.D. Chichén Itzá was influenced, and perhaps invaded, by Toltecs from the city of

Chichén Itzá

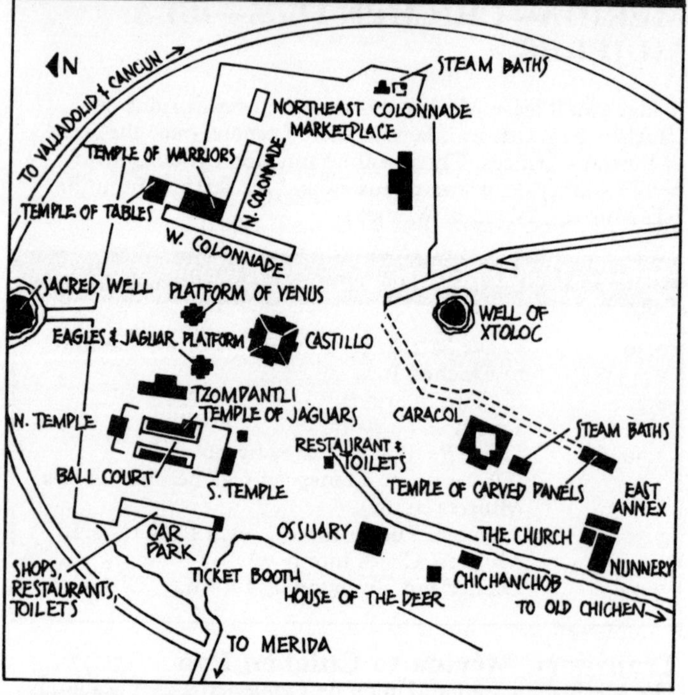

Tula near present-day Mexico City. The Toltecs brought their own style of architecture and the worship of their God-king Quetzalcoátl (the Feathered Serpent), called Kukulcán in Mayan. No one knows whether Quetzalcoátl was a real person who lived at Chichén Itzá or a mythological figure who was already legendary when the Toltecs arrived. The Feathered Serpent was worshipped alongside the Mayan rain god, Chac, and many representations of both gods can be seen at Chichén Itzá.

From about 1200 A.D. to the 16th century, the Mayan-Toltec civil wars may have led to the fall of the Mayan civilisation. When the Spaniards arrived, Chichén's Itzá's people retreated to an island in Lake Petén in Guatemala. They remained there until 1697, when they were defeated and their territory captured by Martín de Ursua, governor of Yucatán.

Once abandoned, the city of Chichén Itzá crumbled into

ruins and was quickly overgrown by jungle. Although never 'lost' like other Mayan cities, Chichén Itzá's significance was unknown until the 1840s. US explorer John Lloyd Stephens discovered the Mayan civilisation at Palenque and other sites, then proved that Chichén Itzá had been part of a vast Mayan empire.

Walk through the Ruins

The ruins are open from 8:00 a.m. to 5:00 p.m. A shop at the gate sells guidebooks, postcards and maps. You can hire a guide (£9) for a 2-hour tour in English, Spanish or French.

Starting at the Castillo (castle) or **Pyramid of Kukulcán**, ascend the main staircase guarded by two gigantic stone heads of the Feathered Serpent. When you reach the top, take the opportunity to orientate yourself with an overview from the summit. This pyramid, built over an earlier Toltec temple, is positioned so that on the days of the spring and autumn equinoxes at 3:00 p.m., seven triangles of light and shadow appear on the side of the ramp, forming the body of a giant serpent. As the sun moves, the serpent appears to descend from the temple.

Next climb the **Temple of the Warriors**, where you'll be greeted by a reclining Chac Mool figure guarded by two more giant serpent heads. Chac Mool represented the messenger of the gods. His carved figure is found at many sites. At the rear of the temple a platform supported by small warrior figures is probably a throne or altar. Below, in the **Temple of 1,000 Columns**, are carved friezes. The original paint is still visible. Across from the columns is a market place complex. To the south-east is a steam-bath used for ritual cleansing, healing and hygiene.

North-west of the Temple of the Warriors, you'll come to the **Platform of Venus**, so called because decorative panels depict Venus emerging from a serpent's mouth. Between the Temple of Venus and the Tzompantli (Wall of Skulls), follow the road to the **Sacred Cenote**, where human sacrifices were made. In 1967, archaeologists dredged the well and found the skeletal remains of over 1,000 victims, mostly children. Also found were copper bells, gold-soled sandals and copal in braziers.

Return to the **Temple of Eagles and Jaguars** to contemplate creatures eating human hearts, then the **Tzompantli**, covered with symbols of death. Continue on to the large and impressive **Ball Court**. The game of *tlachtli* was played by trying to hit a rubber ball through one of the stone hoops without use of the hands. The winning team also 'won' the privilege of being sacrificed to the gods. To the east of the Ball Court, see the beautiful serpent columns of the **Temple of the Jaguars** and the remains of a mural painting.

Returning towards the Castillo, take the path south-west past a much-needed refreshment stand. Continue on the path to the **Ossuary**, where seven tombs were found, the **House of the Deer**, and **Chichanchob** (meaning 'little holes').

Head south-east and cross the path to Old Chichén. See the **Nunnery** complex, so named because it looked to the Spanish like a convent and because it was said that female priests used to live there. The 'church' is decorated with three masks of the rain god, Chac. By now, identifying Kukulcán's dragonlike countenance or Chac's upturned hook nose should be easy. The east face of the Nunnery Annex is marvellously decorated.

On your left is the beautiful and impressive **Caracol.** (snail), a Mayan astronomical observatory. This graceful building is the only circular Mayan structure known. Its four doors open to the four compass points. A small spiral interior staircase, now out of bounds to sightseers, leads to an observatory for the rising and setting of Venus, associated with the deity Quetzalcoátl/Kukulcán.

If you have the time and energy, follow the path to Old Chichén Itzá and visit the **Temple of the Phalluses**, the **Temple of the Atlantes**, and so forth. The entrance at the base of the Castillo to the room of the Red Jaguar opens at 11:00 a.m. Call in on your way out.

Lunch

Take a taxi from the ruins to a restaurant. At the **Pirámide Inn**, not far from the ruins going towards the village of Pisté, a *comida corrida* is less than £2.75 and typical Yucatecan dishes are about £1.30. The use of the swimming pool is included with lunch. The **Restaurant Xay-B** in Pisté also has a pool. The **Villa Archaeológico** in the hotel zone also serves lunch.

Transport: Chichén Itzá to Isla Mujeres

Buses pass through Chichén Itzá for Puerto Juárez every hour on the half-hour. Buy your ticket on the bus. There is a frequent pedestrian ferry service to Isla Mujeres from Puerto Juárez. If you need more help or information, the tourist office information booth at the ruins is open 8:00 a.m.-4:00 p.m. every day except Friday.

Drivers: The car ferry to Isla Mujeres leaves Punta Sam, 5 km beyond Puerto Juárez. You need to be there at 5:00 p.m.

to catch the 5:45 p.m. ferry. It is only a 2-hour drive from Chichén Itzá, so drivers can spend more time in the ruins, take a longer swim or stop at Valledolid to see Cenote Zaci in town.

Isla Mujeres

The island is 5½ miles long and about a mile wide. It's a 45-minute ferry ride from the mainland.

Despite increasing tourism, Isla Mujeres remains a fishing village with a thin and often crumbling resort veneer. The fishing fleet still bobs in the bay, and in the evening fishermen repair nets in doorways. Local restaurant menus vary according to the fleet's catch. Strolling the small streets on a warm tropical evening, glimpse island domestic life through the open doors of small houses.

In 1527, a Spanish expedition, lost at sea for 21 days, sighted the island. Statues of Mayan goddesses guarded the coast, so they named it Island of Women. The only evidence remaining today of pre-Columbian occupation is the small Temple of Ixchel on the southern tip of the island. Isolated Isla Mujeres was a haven for pirates, among them the pirate Mundaca whose hacienda was here.

Accommodation

The **Posada del Mar** is near the beach, and upstairs rooms have views of the sea and the mainland (Av. Rueda Medina 15; Mérida reservation number: 26-04-22). The rather pricey **El Presidente Caribe** (tel. 2-00-29), on the island's prettiest site, is surrounded by water. It has its own aquarium, with turtles and sharks, and a pet pelican. For a comfortable bungalow with fridge and a porch go to **Hotel Kin-Ha** (Carlos Lazo 1).

The best moderate-price deal is the **Hotel Berny** (Juárez por Abasolo, tel. 2-00-25); swimming pool. We also recommend the **Hotel Caracol** (Matamoros 5, tel. 2-01-50). The **Hotel Rocamar** (Nicolas Bravo y Guerrero, tel. 2-01-01) has balconies overlooking the rough sea on the eastern side of the island; make reservations.

The **Hotel Caribe Maya** at Francisco I. Madero 9 (tel. 2-01-90) is a good budget hotel, as is the **Hotel Osario** on the corner of Madero and Juárez (tel. 2-00-18). For the real budget backpacker, the **Hotel Pac-Na** in Matamoros offers dormitory accommodation.

Food

El Peregrino (Francisco I. Madero 8) serves a good meal

and delicious cake. We also recommend the waterfront **Lonchería Miramar**, near the Puerto Juárez ferry dock. For a 'Late '50s Mafia' atmosphere and a decent dinner, try the **Villa del Mar** at Rueda Medina across from the ferry dock. Our favourite hole-in-the-wall is **Carnitas Estilo Michoacán** on the corner of Hidalgo and Abasolo. The **Estrellita Marinera** on the corner of Juárez and Abasolo serves a good breakfast. But the best Mexican breakfast in town is in the market at the stand marked **'El Popular Nacho Beh-El Rey de los Tacos'**, where they serve authentic *conchinita* or *pavo pibil* between 6:00 and 9:00 a.m. (Better to get there early—it goes fast!) Beware the **Tropicana**, an attractive juice and sandwich bar. They charged us an outrageous £1.30 for an ice cream cornet.

Nightlife

La Peña, down from the Hotel Rocamar, has 'Amigo Time' between 6:00 and 7:30 p.m. Nearby **Sergio's** also has a happy hour.

TOUR 18

ISLA MUJERES

You have arrived! No heavy scheduling for today. Relax on the beach.

Suggested schedule

10:00	Late and leisurely breakfast.
11:00	Make for the beach.
2:00	Late and leisurely lunch.
3:00	Laze around the pool or around your room.
5:00	Walk around town. Pick out a boat tour to El Garrafón for tomorrow and make your reservations.
6:00	Happy hour.
7:00	Dinner.
8:00	Hang around on the plaza.

Activities

Several places hire small motorcycles, mopeds or bicycles to buzz around the island. Motorcycles are £7 a day, deposit required. Shop around prices don't vary much, but some machines are nicer than others. Hire windsurfing equipment and/or instruction at Escuela de Windsurfing y Renta de Equipos de Deportes Aquáticos down Coco Beach from Hotel Presidente. Boards are £7 per hour, a 1½-hour lesson £17. They also hire snorkelling equipment, Sunfish sailing boats, Hobiecats, kayaks, air mattresses, beach towels and chairs with umbrellas.

Scuba diving equipment, instruction and guided diving trips are offered by the Diving Shop in front of the ferry dock. The nearby Buceos de México also offers trips to Isla Contoy bird sanctuary, deep-sea fishing and diving. Next door, Isla Mujeres SCL has daily trips to El Garrafón, diving and trips to Isla Contoy. The most economical trips to El Garrafón and other attractions are offered by La Sociedad Coop de Lancheros. Their office is next to the passenger ferry dock. They have a *colectivo* boat trip to El Garrafón every morning at 10:30 a.m. for about £4 per person.

Nightlife

There's something going on around the plaza any evening.

Isla Mujeres

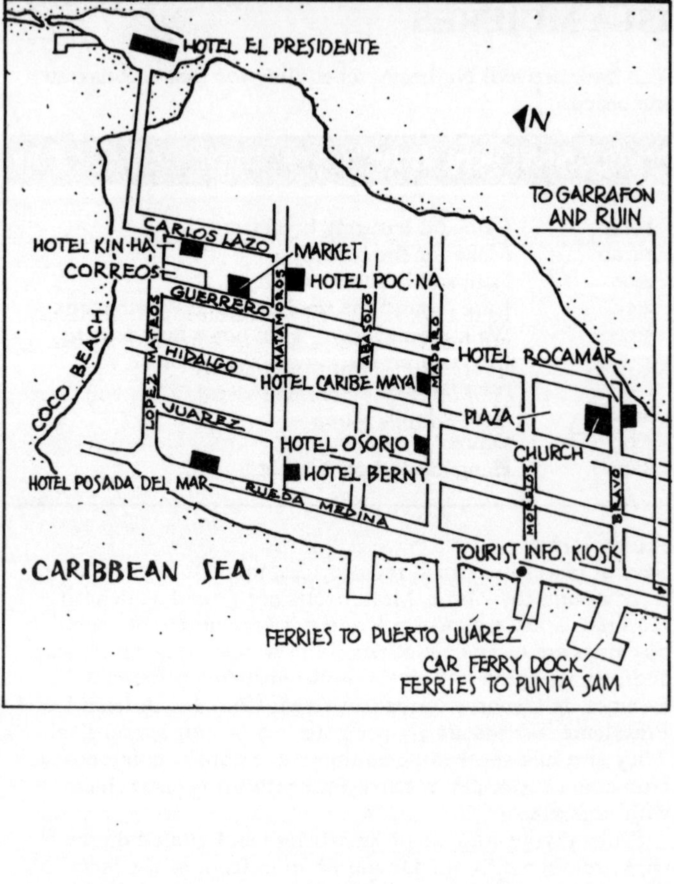

TOUR 19

ISLA MUJERES

More beaches and swimming today, as well as a boat trip to El Garrafón for snorkelling on the coral reef. In the late afternoon you'll visit the Mayan temple on the southern tip of the island.

Suggested schedule

9:00	Breakfast.
10:00	Take boat trip to El Garrafón for snorkelling and lunch. About 4 hours. (Alternative plan: ignore this—back to the beach!)
2:30	Cool off in the pool and write 'Wish you were here' postcards home.
4:30	Hire bicycle and ride to the southern tip of the island to enjoy sunset at the Mayan Templo de Ixchel. (Or: Still at the beach? Hire a moped or taxi later for sunset at Ixchel.)
7:00	Dinner and pack up for early departure tomorrow morning.

Sightseeing highlights

Templo de Ixchel—On the southern tip of the island, this small Mayan lookout tower is perfect for sunset-watching.
Coco Beach—The best swimming beach on the island. Sad to say, the coconut trees that give this beach its name died of disease. The beach runs along the northern end of the island between the Hotel Presidente and the lighthouse.
El Garrafón—This small swimming beach with coral reefs offshore is great for novice snorkellers. Schools of tropical fish thrive in the shelter of the reefs. There are snack bars and snorkel equipment hire. It is a national park, and spear-fishing is not allowed.
Playa Lancheros—This sheltered beach about 5 minutes drive from town on the way to El Garrafón offers sea turtle rides. We've seen the turtles tormented by people climbing on their backs to pose for snapshots. Please have some compassion for this endangered species.

TOUR 20

ISLA MUJERES—COBÁ

Today you will leave your island paradise. Console yourself with a visit to the beautiful lagoon of Xel-ha, and continue on to Tulum, a Mayan ruin on a bluff overlooking the Caribbean. After touring the ruins, you'll proceed to Cobá, where you'll check into a hotel.

Suggested schedule

8:30	Get your well-rested bones up for breakfast.
9:00	Be at the car ferry dock to buy tickets and get in the queue, should there be one.
10:00	Take car ferry to Punta Sam.
11:00	Drive to Xel-ha, lunch.
1:00	Drive to Tulum.
2:15	Tour ruins of Tulum.
4:00	Drive to Cobá.
4:30	Check into hotel.
6:30	Dinner at hotel.

Helpful hints for bus travellers

Catch the 7:00 ferry to Puerto Juárez. Take a city bus from the Puerto Juárez ferry dock into Cancún. Ask to be dropped at the bus station at the corner of Av. Tulum and Av. Uxmal. Get your tickets for Tulum at Autotransportes del Caribe and grab breakfast in the station. Catch the 9:30 bus to Tulum. You'll have a brief 45-minute visit to the ruins and be out at the crossroads in time to catch the noon bus to Cobá. Have lunch in the village, then tour the ruins.

Xel-ha (pronounced 'shell-ha')

A freshwater lagoon mixes with Caribbean salt waters to create this natural aquarium and a snorkeller's paradise. Spear-fishing is prohibited in this national park. In these waters we've seen colourful parrot fish longer and a good deal broader than our daughter. Snorkelling gear can be hired for £2 a day, and underwater cameras, kayaks and a glass-bottomed boat are available. For lunch, try the delicious fried chicken lunch at the **Bar Xel-ha**.

Tulum

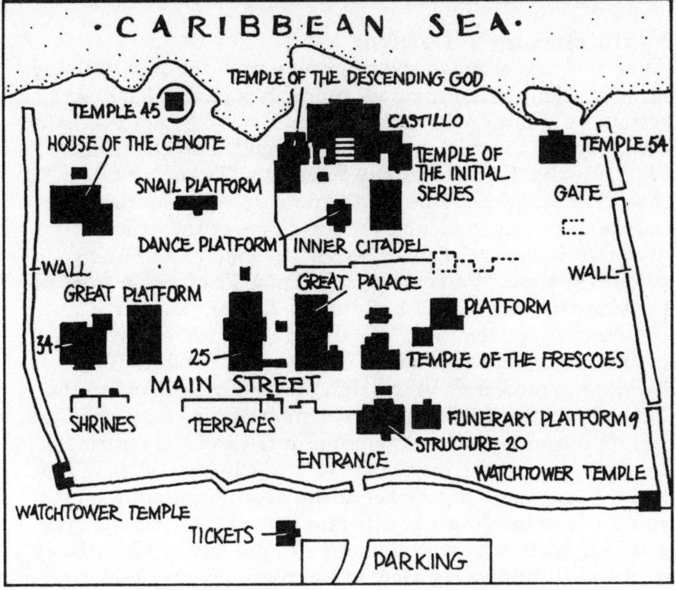

Tulum

Though archaeologists may sniff at this city constructed during the decline of the Mayan civilisation, Tulum holds a powerful magic.

Perched on a 40-foot limestone cliff overlooking the blue-green waters, this walled fortress was first seen by Europeans in 1511. Two shipwreck survivors, Gerónimo de Aguilar and Gonzalo Guerrero, made it to shore and were enslaved by the Mayans. A few years later the chaplain of Juan de Grijalva's expedition described a walled city with towers that looked as large as Seville. Local fishermen told us that they find the entrance to the barrier reef by aligning their boats with the windows of the Castillo.

At the time of the Conquest, a series of forts along this coast protected the Maya from their primitive enemies to the south. The buildings face the south-east, accounting for its ancient name, Zama (place of the sunrise). The modern name, Tulum, means 'wall' and indeed a wall protects the city on three sides.

Ancient Zama must have been an important trading port. Broad stone causeways, an ancient highway system, linked

Tulum to Cobá, Chichén Itzá and Uxmal. Archaeologists date the construction of Zama between 700 A.D. and 1000 A.D.

Walk through Tulum

After you pass through the protective wall, the first building on your right, **Structure 20**, probably a palace, has traces remaining of wall paintings. Beside this building is **Funerary Platform 9**, in which a grave was found. Directly in front of No. 20 is the **Temple of the Frescoes**, Tulum's best-preserved temple. Inside are the remains of some excellent murals. The centre niche over the pillars of the gallery preserves an image of the 'Descending God'. Continuing towards the sea, you come to the Dance Platform in front of the **Castillo**, the largest building at Tulum. The three entrances to the temple at the top of the stairway are flanked by the usual serpent columns of the god Kukulcán. The building immediately to the right of the Castle is called the **Temple of the Initial Series**. Our favourite view of Tulum and its coast is south on the point in front of the remains of **Temple 54**. To the immediate left (north-east) of the Castle is the **Temple of the Descending God**. Continuing north, you come to the **Snail Platform**, named after the shells of giant sea snails that were found here. Zig out to **Temple 45** on the cliff for another view of the coast, and zag back to the **House of the Cenote**, the temple built above the cave that was Tulum's natural storage tank for rainwater. Your vaguely counterclockwise circle takes you to **Structure 34** and the **Great Platform** and **Palace 25** and the **Great Palace**.

The ruins are open from 8:00 a.m. to 5:00 p.m. daily. English-speaking guides are available.

Food and accommodation in Cobá

Determined budget travellers can probably find a room in the village. **El Bocadito** is a small Mayan hotel and restaurant on the side of the main road, just as you enter Cobá. The food is good, and the rooms are clean.

Want to treat yourself to luxury as you near your trip's end? On a lovely lakeshore, the **Hotel Villas Arqueológicas** offers exceptional accommodation—but the price is higher than our usual recommended de luxe hotels. For reservations, write to Hotel Villas Arqueológicas, APDO 710, Cancún, Quintana Roo, Mexico.

TOUR 21

COBÁ—RETURN TO MÉRIDA

Suggested schedule

9:00	Breakfast in hotel.
10:00	Walk to and through Cobá ruins.
1:00	Return to hotel for lunch.
2:00	Drive to Mérida via Valladolid.
5:00	Arrive in Mérida and check into a hotel.
6:00	Perhaps your last dinner in Mexico—Make it a good one!

Helpful hints for bus travellers

A bus leaves for Valladolid at noon; get details from the hotel.

Cobá

Cobá is a Classic site (600-900 A.D.) Its construction style resembles the Mayan ruins of the Petén in Guatemala.

The least-explored and reconstructed ruin on your itinerary, Cobá gives a sense of the tremendous power of the jungle to undo the work of humans. Cobá was once the hub of a network of roads, called *sacbes*, that connected the Mayan peninsular cities. The site extends almost 12 miles and is believed to have more than 6,500 structures. Such is the encroachment of the jungle that less than half of the roads are traceable today, even with aerial mapping.

Walk through Cobá

Immediately upon entering the ruins, take the well-marked pathway to the right to the **Cobá Group**. There is a small ball court and a large pyramid called the Iglesia (church) with a stela (carved stone slab) at the foot of the stairs. Returning to the main path, you'll pass the **Chumuc Mul Group** on your left, still undeveloped. Taking the next well-marked path to the right brings you to the **Las Pinturas Group**, so called because the building on top of the pyramid has paintings on the front. Continuing on the path south, you'll come to Macanxoc Lake and the **Macanxoc Group**, well-preserved stelae. There are also the remains of an old Mayan road. Return to the main path, turn right and you'll come to the **Nohoch Mul Group** on the left. A climb up the 120 steps to

Cobá

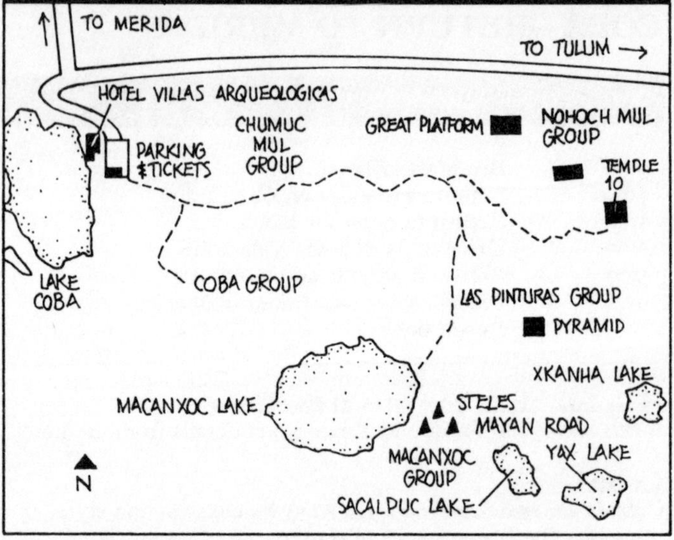

the top of northern Yucatán's tallest pyramid is rewarded by an outstanding view of the surrounding jungle. The temple holds three figures of the Descending God. To the north-west is a view of the **Great Platform**. Descend from the pyramid and visit Stelae 20 in front of **Temple 10**.

Return to Mérida

The new road to Valladolid saves a lot of driving time. Check into your favourite hotel and enjoy a tasty Yucatecan dinner.

This is the end of your itinerary as such. All that is now left is to get home. You will have to return to Mexico City to do so, so you might like to adjust your itinerary slightly, so as to see some of the sights of Mexico City on your way through. You can either do that by taking Tour 1 rather more slowly and leaving part of it for your return or, if you have a little more time, you can try one of the post-tour options.

Whether you stop over on your way through Mexico City or whether you go straight home, you will have had a taste of the real Mexico, and one that will no doubt leave you itching to return!

POST-TOUR OPTIONS

MEXICO CITY

In our itinerary we've only skimmed the surface of what this tremendous city has to offer. If you have extra time, you may want to spend a couple more days here on your way home.

Check the *Mexico City Daily Bulletin* and you'll find 8 pages of gallery and exhibition listings—something for everybody. The Federal Power Commission Technology Museum, for example, recently exhibited works from the northern state of Coahuila. We could kick ourselves for not getting to the Museum of Corruption while it was open.

Not listed in the *Daily Bulletin*, but of particular interest to Diego Rivera fans, is the Secretaria de Educación Pública building with over 200 Rivera murals. At Calle Argentina 28, not far from the Zócalo, the building is open from 8:00 a.m. to 8:00 p.m., Mon.-Fri.

Coyoacán and University City

A 30-minute taxi journey south from the Zócalo, the National University of Mexico is the oldest school of higher learning in the Americas, chartered in 1551. The buildings themselves are monumental works of art, covered with murals designed by Juan O'Gorman, David Siqueiros, Jose Morado and Francisco Helguera.

Fifteen minutes away in Coyoacán is the Frida Kahlo Museum (at the corner of Allende and Londres at 247), the former home of Frida Kahlo and her husband, Diego Rivera. Visit the Anahuacalli-Diego Rivera Museum, displaying the artist's collection of pre-Columbian art (Calle Museo 150). Leon Trotsky's home is in the same area at Viena 45.

Xochimilco (pronounced So-chee-meel-co)

Go on a Sunday when these floating gardens are crowded with boats full of families out for picnics. There are boatloads of musicians for hire by the song or by the hour, or you can just enjoy the music in passing. You can bargain for a barge to float you through the canals—a sample of the intricate waterways of Tenochtitlán before the conquest, when landfills of mud and reed were used for cultivation. Taxi is the easiest way to get there.

La Villa de Guadalupe

After the Conquest, the Archbishop of Mexico ordered all

pagan shrines destroyed. These included the shrine of the Aztec goddess of earth and corn, Tonantzin (the virgin and little mother) on Tepeyac Hill near the capital. On 9 December, 1531, on this same hill, the Virgin Mary appeared to Juan Diego, a poor Indian convert. She told him that she wanted a church built on the site. And so this dark-skinned Virgin replaced the Aztec goddess.

In 1976, a huge modern basilica was built to exhibit Juan Diego's cloak miraculously imprinted with the Virgin's image. The original Spanish church nearby is now a museum. This is Mexico's most sacred shrine. Take Metro Line 3 to the Basílica stop.

TAXCO

Taxco is only a little over 100 miles (3 hours' drive) from Mexico City, in the state of Guerrero, and can be reached easily by bus or hire car. The town is famous for silver jewellery. Sterling silver will be stamped with the number 925, signifying that it is 92.5% pure silver.

The town is built on a mountainside. Be prepared to climb steep, narrow cobblestone streets. If you're driving, park on or near the road that runs along the bottom of the town. Taxco is a tourist town, with an array of restaurants and hotels to choose from. Guides steer you to shops that pay them commissions, raising the price of what you buy. The town is not large, so there's no problem exploring it on your own. Explore the market in the lower section of town. It's built in layers up the hill, some of it on the stairways.

Getting there: If you're driving, take the toll road (95D) out of Mexico City toward Cuernavaca. Head south toward Acapulco until you see signs for Taxco. To go by bus, take the Metro to Mexico City's Terminal Central de Autobuse del Sur (Calzada Tlalpan 2205, Taxquena Metro station). Estrella de Oro is the first-class service to Taxco. Flecha Roja offers second-class service. You can also take a tour. Check with a travel agency or ask at your hotel.

PACIFIC BEACHES

Manzanillo

Mexico's major west coast port has recently become a tourist centre. This crowded, hot little town contrasts with an incredible jet-set resort, Las Hadas ('the fairies'), located across Manzanillo Bay. Built by Bolivian tin magnate Antenor Patino, Las Hadas is worth visiting for a drink and a swim even if you don't intend to stay there.

You'll find a number of hotels and bungalows in the Las Brisas beach area north of town along Manzanillo Bay. The beach at Las Brisas is steep and not as good for swimming as other beaches a little farther north on Santiago Bay, which also offers several hotel choices.

Manzanillo can be reached by air from most major cities in Mexico. The international airport is 30 miles north of town. *Colectivos* and taxis, as well as local buses, make frequent trips from the airport into the city and to nearby resorts. You can also reach Manzanillo by train, with daily departures from Guadalajara, or on numerous first- and second-class bus services. It's about a six-hour journey by car or bus from Guadalajara; the train takes twice as long.

Barra de Navidad and Melaque (San Patricio)

Melaque and Barra de Navidad are two small beach towns about 35 miles up the coast from Manzanillo. They are so close together as to be practically one town, and it's a pleasant walk along the beach between the two. At weekends and holidays, people from Guadalajara come in droves. During the week it's usually quiet. The beaches are fine, and moderately priced hotels, bungalows and good seafood restaurants abound. Barra has more and better restaurants. Melaque is at the more sheltered end of the bay, its beach is less sloped and the water is calmer for swimming.

The beach restaurants of Barra are a good place to experience Seafood Sunday. Huge extended families and groups of friends gather for an afternoon of eating, drinking and music provided by local mariachi bands. You may be offered drinks and plates of shrimp and other delicacies. Mexicans are amazingly hospitable and often invite passing tourists to join their picnics and family get-togethers.

Getting there: There is a frequent service by bus, *colectivo* or taxi from Manzanillo International Airport to both towns. Buses also run from Guadalajara (about a 6-hour trip) and Puerto Vallarta (about 3 hours). The towns are an easy bus or taxi journey from Manzanillo. *Colectivos* and local buses run frequently between Barra and Melaque.

Puerto Vallarta

With a population of 120,000, Puerto Vallarta (or 'P.V.' as local expatriates call it) is one of Mexico's most popular tourist centres. Prices are high, and it can be crowded. Tourism has brought a wide selection of excellent restaurants and lots of nightlife, as well as a large (if somewhat overpriced) selection of arts and crafts from all over Mexico.

The small beach towns of Sayutla and Rincon de Guayabitos a few miles north of Puerto Vallarta offer a less expensive, more tranquil haven. There's not much happening except the sea.

Getting there: There is a frequent bus service from Guadalajara and Tepic to P.V. The roads are in good condition. There is an international airport with flights arriving from many Mexican cities.

Ferry to Baja California

Note: The ferry to and from Baja has been out of service, but rumour has it that it will soon be back in operation.

From Puerto Vallarta, you can continue by ferry to Cabo San Lucas on the southern end of the Baja California peninsula. (Note: Hotels and meals are considerably more expensive in Baja than on the Mexican mainland.) The ferry, operated by the Mexican government, leaves Puerto Vallarta twice a week for the 24-hour trip to Cabo San Lucas. Check at the ferry terminal on the northern outskirts of Puerto Vallarta for current schedules and ask when to purchase tickets.

We have taken this ferry many times and the procedure has never been the same twice. The ferry takes cars as well as foot passengers and the number of cabins is limited, so queue early to ensure that you get one. Cabins come in three classes: *Especial*, the most luxurious with bath and sitting space; *Cabina*, with two bunks and a bath; and *Turista*, with two bunks and the bath down the hall. If you are travelling alone you may be asked to share a cabin with a stranger of the same sex. If there are no berths available you can go *Salón* class but this requires sitting up all night in an airline-type chair or throwing down a sleeping bag and sleeping on the deck. Meals are served in both a dining room and a cafeteria. The meals in the dining room are acceptable but expensive by Mexican standards and the cafeteria meals are not recommended. We always pack a lunch and take fruit, snacks, fruit juice and soft drinks. There are a couple of bars on the ship, but they are not always open. On some voyages we have been treated to live music in the bar and dancing, quite a challenge when the ship is rolling.

The ferry trip with cabin is very inexpensive. On our last trip the *Cabina* class for two cost only £4.

PRACTICAL EXTRAS

CULTURE SHOCK

A Mexican travel experience can be overwhelming. Total immersion in a foreign language can be like a plunge into icy water. Help! you gulp as you grope madly for your phrasebook. Then you realise you took the wrong turning a few streets back and you're hopelessly lost . . .

Sudden panic is one form of culture shock. If it happens to you, sit down on a park bench or in a restaurant. Sit on the kerb if you have to. There's nothing like getting your body a little closer to the earth ('grounding') to calm you down. Have a familiar Coca-Cola or cup of coffee and a snack, and sit back and watch life going on around you for a little while. This may be the perfect opportunity to observe everyday Mexican life. Practice your Spanish on the little boy selling *chicles* (chewing gum). Get out your map and phrasebook and ask a waiter or passerby for directions.

Homesickness is also a form of culture shock. If you've never been homesick before, you may not even recognise the symptoms. A friend, new to Mexico, had been unhappy and out of sorts for several days. He was suddenly himself again, while pushing a trolley through a shopping centre; the familiarity of the surroundings had brought about the transformation.

Stay in hotels you like. If your budget calls for the cheaper hotel, but you don't feel comfortable when you look at the room, splash out. Take a room you like better in a slightly more expensive hotel. Your hotel room is your temporary home, your retreat from stress, a place to nurture yourself—so treat yourself right.

Long distance telephone calls: You can often make calls abroad from your hotel room, or at least from reception. To phone home during your trip, we recommend you ask at your hotel for the particulars.

SPEAKING SPANISH

Language is like money. There's a great difference between a small amount and none at all.

If you have studied Spanish before, brush up. Take a class with a Spanish-speaking instructor or hire a free-lance tutor. If that's impractical, get some language study materials from your library or bookshop. Among the best self-teaching books is *An Essential Course in Modern Spanish* by H. Ramsden (Nelson). Starting at least a month to six weeks before your trip, work on your Spanish for an hour every day.

To practise hearing and speaking Spanish, try Berlitz's *Spanish for Travellers* (Latin American edition—60-minute cassette and phrasebook), or the BBC's *Dígame* course in Spanish (BBC Publications). Both are great for joggers or for popping into your car cassette player while you drive to work.

Most important, *try to communicate!* Any effort at communication will be richly rewarded, as Mexicans meet your attempts with a sympathetic ear and a big smile.

On a bus trip through Mexico a friend was doing his utmost to be polite and communicative with the Indians. One day as we struggled towards the exit on a packed bus, Steve overheard him exclaiming, '*Escusado! Escusado!*' to alarmed-looking passengers. He thought he was saying 'Excuse me!' but was actually calling out 'Toilet! Toilet!'

Pronunciation guide

Once you learn the vowel sounds in Spanish, you can pronounce most words you see written. Each vowel has only one sound, and the sounds of most consonants are similar to English.

Vowels:
A is a 'short a' (as in F**A**THER)
E sounds like 'eh' (as in **E**RROR)
I sounds like 'ee' (as in POL**I**CE)
O is a 'long o' (as in G**O**)
U sounds like 'oo' (as in R**U**IN)

Consonants that are different from English:
ñ sounds like 'ny' (cañon = 'canyon')
ll sounds like 'y' (llama = 'yama')
rr is trilled
g sounds like 'h' (except when followed by a 'u') 'gu . . .' is pronounced like an English hard 'g'
h is always silent (hola = 'ola')
qu sounds like an English 'k' (que = 'kay')

Pronounce all syllables distinctly. Words ending in a vowel are accented on the next-to-last syllable, and those ending in a consonant are usually accented on the last syllable. A written accent mark shows that the word is accented differently from this general rule.

l handy phrases

de está . . . ?
. Quiero un boleto a . . .
much is a ticket to . . . ? ¿Cuánto cuesta un boleto a . . . ?
I want to make a reservation. Quiero hacer una reservación.
Which bus service goes to _______ ? ¿Cuál línea tiene servicio a _______ ?
What is the number of the bus? ¿Qué es el numero del autobús?
What time does the plane (bus, train) leave? ¿A qué hora sale el avión (camión, tren)?
Where does it leave from? ¿De dónde sale?
Where does this bus go? ¿Dónde va este autobús?
Does this bus go to _______ ? ¿Se va este autobús a _______ ?
How many hours to _______ ? ¿Cuántas horas a _______ ?
How much time do we have here? ¿Cuánto tiempo tenemos aquí?
I want to get off at the corner (. . . here). Quiero bajar en la esquina (. . . aquí).
What will you charge to take me to _______ ? ¿Cuánto me cobra llevarme a _______ ?
I lost my baggage. Se me perdió mi equipaje.
Where are you going? ¿A dónde va usted?
It leaves at . . . Sale a las . . .
ticket office caja (or) taquilla
reservation reservación
reserved seat asiento reservado (or) numerado
arrival llegada
departure salida
every hour cada hora
every half hour cada media hora
daily diario
passenger pasajero
driver chófer
line (or) company línea (or) compañía
to get on subir
to get off bajar
airport aeropuerto
bus autobús (or) camión
city bus (servicio) urbano

train tren
railway ferrocarril
aeroplane avión
first class primera clase
second class segunda clase
taxi taxi, libre, coche (or) combi (or) coche de sitio
taxi stand sitio
bus station terminal (or) estación de autobús (or) central de camiones
bus stop parada
railway station estación de ferrocarril
ticket boleto

Days of the week

Monday Lunes
Tuesday Martes
Wednesday Miércoles
Thursday Jueves
Friday Viernes
Saturday Sábado
Sunday Domingo

Numbers

1 uno
2 dos
3 tres
4 cuatro
5 cinco
6 seis
7 siete
8 ocho
9 nueve
10 diez
11 once
12 doce
13 trece
14 catorce
15 quince
16 diez y seis
17 diez y siete
18 diez y ocho
19 diez y nueve
20 veinte
21 veinte y uno
22 veinte y dos
23 veinte y tres
24 veinte y cuatro
30 treinta
40 cuarenta
50 cincuenta
60 sesenta
70 setenta
80 ochenta
90 noventa
100 cien (or) ciento
1,000 mil

Colours

black negro
white blanco
red rojo
orange naranja

yellow amarillo
green verde
blue azul
brown marrón
pink rosa

Time

What is the time? ¿Que hora es?
two o'clock las dos
half past three las tres y media
a quarter past four las cuatro y cuarto
a quarter to five las cinco menos cuarto
five past six las seis y cinco

Hotels

Do you know of a cheap hotel? ¿Conoce usted un hotel económico?
I would like a room. Quiero un cuarto.
for _______ days para _______ dias
Do you have a room for two? ¿Hay un cuarto para dos personas?
a room with bath un cuarto con baño
with meals con comidas
I want a quiet room, inside. Quiero un cuarto sin ruido, adentro.
I want an upstairs room. Quiero un cuarto arriba.
Do you have parking? ¿Hay estacionamiento?
Is the car safe? ¿Está seguro el coche?
Is there a night watchman at the car park? ¿Hay un velador en el estacionamiento?
Do you have ice? ¿Hay hielo?
hotel hotel
motel motel
inn posada
bath (or) bathroom baño
room cuarto
key llave
blanket cobija
double bed cama de matrimonio
shower regadera
hot water agua caliente
fan ventilador (or) abanico
air conditioned aire acondicionado
manager gerente (or) dueño
dining room comedor
bar bar

swimming pool alberca (or) piscina
noise ruido

Post office, telegraph, telephone, bank

I want _______ stamps for England. Quiero _______ estampillas (timbres) para Inglaterra.
Three airmail envelopes, please. Tres sobres aereos, por favor.
I would like to send a telegram to _______ Quiero mandar una telegrama a _______
I want to phone England. Quiero llamar a Inglaterra.
The number is . . . El número es . . .
What time does the bank open? ¿A qué hora abre el banco?
Can one cash a traveller's cheque? ¿Se puede cambiar un cheque de viajero?
What is the exchange rate? ¿A cómo se cambia?
post office correos
general delivery lista de correos
letter carta
address dirección
envelope sobre
stamp estampilla (or) timbre
post card tarjeta
telegraph office telégrafos
telegram telegrama
telephone office oficina de teléfonos
telephone teléfono
to call llamar
a call una llamada
number número
operator operador
long distance larga distancia
collect por cobrar
person to person persona a persona
station to station a quién contesta
credit card tarjeta de crédito
Hello! Ola! (or) Bueno!
money dinero
change feria, cambio (or) suelto
cheque cheque
traveller's cheque cheque de viajero
currency (Mexican) moneda nacional
pounds sterling libras esterlinas
note billete
bank banco
teller's window caja

signature firma
bureau de change casa de cambio

MEXICAN FOOD

Health: We once overheard some tourists in a caravan park offering their neighbours a melon that they had soaked in water with a purifying tablet, saying they 'thought it would be okay'. We've met Americans, travelling in giant trailers, who brought freezers full of food under the mistaken impression that it was unsafe to eat in Mexico. Some even brought a full water supply and went home when it ran out.

Only raw fruits and vegetables that you can't peel need to be soaked in water with water purification drops. In better restaurants you can trust the cleanliness, but if you want to be fanatically careful for the duration of the trip, you can keep off salads.

Drink mineral water with your meals. *Agua mineral sin sabor* (mineral water without flavour) is a refreshing sugarless beverage. Brand names include Peñafiel, Tehuacan and Etiqueta Azul.

Tortillas: The *tortilla* is universal in Mexico, and, once you learn that it often forms the bulk of a simple meal, you will leave a restaurant satisfied. You usually get a huge pile of *tortillas* with your meal, and you're free to ask for more. They also serve as eating utensils. It's considered polite and normal to scoop up your beans with *tortillas*, or create *tacos* out of anything on your plate using your salad as garnish. If you don't like *tortillas,* you can usually get *bolillos*, French-style rolls. At worst, you'll be served *pan Bimbo*, the Wonder Bread of Mexico.

Every town has one or more *tortillerías* mass-producing *tortillas* for sale early every morning to people who line up with their baskets, towels and buckets at hand to carry home the daily stack. The *tortillería* of one small village we visit often now processes 5 tons of *masa* (corn flour) every day.

Comida Corrida: Restaurants throughout Mexico serve an afternoon dinner 'special' called the *comida corrida*. Often the menu of the *comida corrida* will be posted outside the restaurant. With at least two choices in each course, it is a bargain. The *comida corrida* is traditionally served between 1:00 p.m. and 4:00 p.m. The *comida corrida* is prepared ahead of time. If you're in a hurry, it's the best choice.

Meats: The word *bistec* comes from the English word

'beefsteak'. In Mexico it means a slice or steak of any meat or fish, so you can get *bistec de puerco*, for instance—'beefsteak of pork'. *Chuleta* means 'chop' and may be of *res* (beef) or *puerco* (pork). A *milanesa* is a thin steak of beef or pork, breaded and fried. *Asado* or *a la parilla* is 'grilled', and *al carbón* is 'charcoal grilled'.

Tamales: *Tamales* come in many forms. (It is one *tamal*, two or more *tamales.*) In the highlands the wrapping around the *masa* (dough) is usually a cornhusk, in the tropical regions a banana leaf is used. Fillings range from sweet to meat.

Chiles: Mexico has an incredible variety of chili peppers, and names for the same chili vary regionally. The common chilis are:

Chile poblano—a long, dark green chili used for *chiles rellenos* (stuffed chilis). Fairly piquant to bell-pepper mild.

Chile jalapeño—fresh or pickled and tinned. Approach with caution.

Chile serrano—smaller and thinner than a *jalapeño,* it is served in the same way and is commonly pickled and tinned. Fresh *serranos* can be real smokers!

Chile habanero (Yucatán)—beware, extremely piquant. Looks like a miniature bell pepper, but that's where the resemblance ends. Its delicious and unique flavour should be tasted with extreme care.

Chile chipotle—a smoked *jalapeño* in a rich dark sauce. It has a unique flavour, usually quite piquant.

Salsas (hot sauces): Mexican hot sauces fall into several categories. Uncooked *salsa* is made of chopped tomatoes, onions and fresh chili peppers and *cilantro* (fresh coriander or Chinese parsley). Cooked, this *salsa* is called *salsa ranchera.*

Salsas are also made from dried chilis. Brick red and thin, they may have seeds floating in them.

A common *salsa* uses the *tomatillo* (green husk tomato) as a base and may be either cooked or raw. Commercially bottled *salsas* come in every imaginable flavour.

Will the food be too 'hot' to eat? If you don't like hot chilis and *salsas*, don't despair—you'll be able to eat in Mexico. If you don't eat piquant food, be careful of *moles, chiles rellenos, enchiladas (enchiladas suisas* are usually safe), and anything with *ranchero* (country style) attached to the name.

Remedies: If you bite into something too hot, take a pinch of salt. It's better to drink something hot, rather than cold, to wash away the effects. Remember, unseen chili juices remain on your hands and can burn other parts of your body.

Central Mexico food specialities

Carnitas ('little meats') are pork cooked in huge cannibal pots. You will see these big black pots in the streets of many small towns in Central Mexico; we can never resist stopping and buying some *carnitas*. Ask for *carne maciza* (lean meat) and avoid the fat, ears, tails and other delicacies so dear to many Mexicans. *Carnitas* make great picnic food.

Cabrito Asado: Very young kid goat grilled over mesquite coals. So good it's definitely worth trying.

Pozole: This Mexican version of hominy soup may contain kidneys, livers and other meat.

Mole Poblano: There are many different flavours of *mole* in Mexico (*mole* means 'sauce' or 'gravy'), but *mole poblano* is the most famous. It contains bitter chocolate as well as an indescribable combination of spices, herbs and hot chilis. It is an acquired taste.

Filete Tampiqueño: This is a 'Mexican mixed grill', consisting of a grilled flank steak served with *enchiladas*, refried beans, *guacamole* and rice.

Caldo Tlalpeño: This delicious soup of chicken and uncooked avocado, flavoured with the smoky chili *chipotle*, is often slightly piquant, but delicious.

A note to vegetarians: Most larger cities and towns have at least one vegetarian restaurant and often a natural foods shop where you can buy whole grains, etc. Many restaurants serve meatless meals: cheese *enchiladas, chiles rellenos,* and of course the old standby, beans and *tortillas*. At the market, buy fresh fruits and vegetables, fruit drinks, fresh bread and cheese.

Yucatán food specialities

The food of the Yucatán is a melting pot of Mayan, Caribbean, European and Middle Eastern cooking styles.

Sopa de Lima: This famous Yucatán chicken soup gets its unique flavour from the juice of the *lima agria* (bitter lime).

Cochinita Pibil: Pit barbecued piglet coated with *achiote* and bitter orange juice sauce. It is made into soft *tacos* or big sandwiches with *pan frances* (French bread). Addictive.

Pavo Pibil: Turkey cooked by the same method as described above.

Huevos Motuleños: This popular breakfast dish is similar to *huevos rancheros*, but more elaborate.

Huevos Malagueños: Eggs baked with shrimp and tomato sauce, garnished with asparagus.

Venado: Venison is commonly served in rural Yucatán restaurants.

Seafood

Shellfish: *Camarones al mojo de ajo* (fresh shrimp sautéed in the shell with lots of garlic) is wonderful. Steve eats the crispy shells too. *Camarones al diablo* are similar, but with hot sauce, hence the name 'of the devil'. If you prefer the simple flavour of fresh shrimp, order them *al natural*.

Seafood cocktails abound. Order them with or without *picante* and other flavourings. Mexicans often add *cilantro* (fresh coriander or Chinese parsley) to their seafood cocktails. If you have an aversion to this strong-tasting herb, be sure to order your cocktail *sin cilantro*.

Fish: *Huachinango* (red snapper) is a popular dish in restaurants everywhere. It is often served in *mojo de ajo* (garlic sauce), *entero* (whole fried fish) or *filete asado* (grilled fillet). *Huachinango a la veracruzana* (red snapper Veracruz style) is fried and then simmered in a sauce of fresh tomatoes, onions, olives and capers. Other common fish are *sierra* (mild-flavoured mackerel), *mojarra* (perch-like fish, often fried whole) and *lisa* (mullet), boney but tasty.

Pulpo en Su Tinta: Octopus in its ink is for the adventurous only. Great flavour if you can get past the tentacles.

Food vocabulary

I'm hungry Tengo hambre
I'm thirsty Tengo sed
What is there to eat? (. . . to drink?) ¿Qué hay para comer? (. . . para beber?)
Are there beans? (. . . eggs?) ¿Hay frijoles? (. . . huevos?)
I want . . . Quiero . . .
We want . . . Queremos . . .
The bill, please. La cuenta, por favor.
We want to pay separately. Queremos pagar aparte.
The meal was very good. La comida estuvo muy sabrosa.
restaurant restaurante, comedor, lonchería (or) fonda
menu menú
plate plato
an order un orden
snack antojito (or) botana
dessert postre
beverage bebida
fork tenedor
spoon cuchara
knife cuchillo

cup taza
glass vaso
napkin servilleta
toothpick palillo
purified water agua purificada

Breakfast desayuno
bacon tocino
butter mantequilla
eggs huevos
  scrambled eggs huevos revueltos
  fried eggs huevos fritos
  hardboiled eggs huevos hervidos duros
  softboiled eggs huevos tibios (or) huevos pasados por agua
hot cakes hot kakes
jam mermelada
margarine margarina
toast pan tostado (or) pan dorado

Fruit fruta
fruit salad ensalada de frutas
fruit juice jugo de fruta
apple manzana
banana platano
melon melón
grapefruit toronja
lemon limón
lime lima
orange naranja
orange juice jugo de naranja
pineapple piña
strawberry fresa
watermelon sandía

Vegetables verduras (or) legumbres
avocado aguacate
beans frijoles
  refried beans refritos
  boiled beans frijoles de olla
cabbage col (or) repollo
cauliflower coliflor
corn maíz
lettuce lechuga
onion cebolla
peas chícharos
rice arroz

salad ensalada
tomato tomate (or) jitomate

Bread pan
roll bolillo
sandwich sanwich (or) torta

Beverages bebidas
beer cerveza
chocolate milk Chocomil (brand name)
  hot chocolate leche caliente con chocolate
coffee café
  coffee with cream café con crema
  black coffee café americano
  coffee 'au lait' café con leche (mixed with hot milk)
  Mexican-style coffee café de olla (with cinnamon and sugar, boiled in a clay pot)
cream crema
milk leche
mineral water agua mineral
  without flavouring sin sabor
  non-carbonated sin gas
soft drink refresco
tea té
  black tea té negro
  camomile herbal tea té de manzanillo
  lemon grass herbal tea té de limón
wine vino de uva
  white wine vino blanco
  red wine vino tinto

Meat carne
steak bistec
chop chuleta
beef res
chicken pollo
  chicken breast pechuga de pollo
  chicken leg pierna de pollo
fish pescado
ham jamón
hamburger hamburguesa
liver hígado
pork puerco
  pork chop chuleta de puerco
sausage salchicha
spicy Mexican sausage chorizo

broth caldo
soup sopa
noodles fideos
spaghetti, macaroni espageti, macarrónes (or) pasta
black pepper pimienta negra
garlic ajo
salt sal
sugar azucar

CRAFTS AND FOLK ART

One of Mexico's great natural wonders is its enormous variety of handmade crafts and art. There isn't a medium that the Mexican artisan has not explored—clay, wood, gourds, metals, straw, papier-mâché, bark, seashells, textiles. The quality is equally varied, from Tijuana tat to exquisite craftsmanship.

Fonart is a chain of Mexican government craft and folk art stores. Prices are controlled, and you may find better deals than at retail shops.

Vendors will claim there isn't a shred of acrylic fibre in all of Mexico, or any polyester—it's all *pura lana* or *pura algodón* (pure wool, pure cotton). In the case of wool, look for the tell-tale glitter of acrylic blend in the sunshine. Polyester blends usually have a smoother texture than pure cotton, which is often a little wrinkled. If you're buying cotton clothing, remember it will shrink unless the cloth has been pre-shrunk.

In the Market-place

How much is it? ¿Cuánto cuesta?
I can't pay that much. No puedo pagar tanto.
I can't pay more than _______ No puedo pagar más que _______
It's very pretty. Es muy bonita.
It's too big (small). Es demasiado grande (pequeño).
I don't like the colour. No me gusta el color.
Will it shrink? ¿Va a recoger?
Won't the colours run? ¿No se manchan los colores?
Do you have it in pink (blue)? ¿Hay en color rosa (azul)?
I don't want it, thank you. No lo quiero, gracias.
I'm looking for a _______ Busco un _______
What size? ¿Qué tamaño?
Won't you sell it to me for _______ ? ¿No me lo vende a _______ ?

Where do they sell _______ ? ¿Dónde se venden _______ ?
market mercado (or) tianguis
shop tienda
clothing ropa
pottery cerámica
weaving tejido
wool lana
cotton algodón
acrylic acrílico
hammock hamaca
basket canasta
folk art, crafts artesanía
mask máscara
jewellery shop joyería

Market days

Mexico City:
La Lagunilla—indoor market, daily. Outdoor flea market in surrounding streets on Saturdays and Sundays.
Mercado Merced—daily
Mercado Sonora—daily
Ciudadela—daily
Zochimilco, D.F.—Sat. & Thur.

San Miguel de Allende—indoor market daily, street market Sunday and Thursday, used clothing market Tuesday.

Guanajuato—daily

Pátzcuaro—Friday and Sunday

Oaxaca area:
Oaxaca city market—Saturday
Tlacolula de Matamoros—Sunday
Mitla—Sunday
Miahuatlán—Monday
Soledad Etla—Tuesday
San Pedro y San Pablo Etla—Wednesday
Ejutla—Wednesday
Zimatlán de Alvarez—Wednesday
Zaachila—Thursday
Ocotlán de Morelos—Friday

San Cristóbal area:
San Cristóbal de las Casas—daily
San Juan de Chamula—Sunday
Zinacantán—Sunday

Amatenango—Sunday
Tenejapa—Thursday

Mérida—daily

Isla Mujeres—daily

FIESTAS

January
6—**Día de los Reyes** (Day of the Kings), all Mexico, Christmas gifts given.
17—Blessings of farm animals and pets.
20—**Día de San Sebastián**, Guanajuato.
20—**Fiesta de San Sebastián**, San Juan de Chamula, Chiapas

February
2—**Candelario** (Candlemas, midpoint between winter solstice and spring equinox), all Mexico.
2—Native dances, Santa Maria del Tule, Oaxaca.
5—**Constitution Day**, all Mexico, national holiday.
7-8—**Festival of the Lord of Rescue** (local saint), Tzintzuntzan, Michoacán, fair with dances.
Week before Ash Wednesday—**Carnival**, most spectacular in: San Juan de Chamula, Chiapas; Tenejapa, Chiapas; Zaachila, Oaxaca; Isla Mujeres, Quintana Roo; Mérida, Yucatán; Manzanillo, Colima; and Veracruz, Veracruz.

March
First Friday—**Festival of the Lord of the Conquest**, San Miguel de Allende.
21—**Benito Juárez's Birthday**, national holiday.
Week before Easter—**Semana Santa**, all Mexico. Good Friday is particularly good in Pátzcuaro, Mich., as are: Maundy Thursday in Tzintzuntzan, Mich; All-week celebrations in San Miguel de Allende, Gto.; Corpus Christi—Mexico City, children bring baskets of fruit and food to the Cathedral to be blessed; Good Friday—Ixtalalapa, D.F., enactment of the crucifixion; Tuesday of Passion Week—Xochimilco flower fair.

May
1—**Labour Day**, national holiday.
3—**Day of the Cross**, all Mexico. Xochimilco, D.F., has a competition of flower-decorated altars. Big celebration in

San Juan de Chamula, Chiapas.
5—**Cinco de Mayo**, all Mexico, national holiday celebrating the defeat of the French at Pueblo. Mexico City has a reenactment of the battle.
15—Animals decorated, all Mexico.

June
10—**Día de San Antonio**: the following Sunday San Miguel de Allende celebrates this saint with the dances of *Los Locos* (the madmen) and a fair.
23—**Fiesta de La Olla** (Festival of the Pot), Guanajuato, Gto., serenades and dances.
24—**Día de San Juan**, San Juan de Chamula, Chiapas, ritual horse races, processions.

July
First Wednesday in July—**Día de la Preciosa Sangre de Cristo** (Precious Blood of Christ), Teotitlán del Valle, Oax., processions and dances.
3—**Fiesta**, Oaxaca, Oax.
Third & Last Mondays in July—Lunes del Cerro, Oaxaca, Oax., Indian dances honouring the goddess of corn so she may bless the harvest.
16—**Día de Nuestra Señora de Carmen**, traditional dances in the *barrio* of San Angel on the outskirts of Mexico City.
24—**Fiesta de San Juan**, Palenque, Chiapas.
25—**Día de Santiago Apóstal**, Tenejapa, Chiapas.
25—**Día de Santiago Apóstal**, Amatenango del Valle, Chiapas.
17-25—**Día de San Cristóbal**, San Cristóbal de las Casas, Chiapas, pilgrimages, candlelit vigils.
25—All Mexico, national holiday.

August
4—**Fiesta de Santo Domingo de Guzman**, Palenque, Chiapas.
10—**Día de San Lorenzo**, Zinacantán, Chiapas.
13—Mexico City, D.F., dances celebrating the defence of the Aztec city of Tenochtitlán against the Spanish.
15—**Festival of Our Lady of the Cibary**, Santa Clara del Cobre, Mich., fair and dances.
15—**Festival of the Assumption of the Virgin**, Santa Maria del Tule, Oax., procession, floral wreaths.
30—**Día de Santa Rosa**, San Juan de Chamula, Chiapas, music.
31—Blessing of the animals, Oaxaca.

September

1-5—**Fiesta de Santo Domingo**, Palenque, Chiapas.
8—**Festival of the Birth of the Virgin Mary**, Teotitlán del Valle, Oax., procession and dances.
14—**Charro Day** (gentlemen cowboys), all Mexico.
16—**Independence Day**, all Mexico, celebration of the beginning of the War of Independence; fireworks and parades in Mexico City and San Miguel de Allende, Gto.
24—**Fiesta del Barrio de la Merced**, San Cristóbal de las Casas, Chiapas.
29—**Día de San Miguel**, celebrated the following Saturday in San Miguel de Allende, Gto., bullfighting, fireworks, dances.

October

1-5—**Ferria de San Francisco**, Amatenango del Valle, Chiapas.
First Sunday in October—**Festival of Our Lady of the Rosary**, San Juan de Chamula, Chiapas, music, costumes, dancing, market.
6-8—**Feria de la Virgen del Rosario**, San Juan de Chamula, Chiapas.
12—**Columbus Day**, national holiday.

November

1-2—**Day of the Dead**, all Mexico, particularly spectacular on the island of Janitzio, Mich.
13—**Día de San Diego**, celebrated the following Sunday, Mexico City D.F., costumes, dances, fireworks.
20—**Anniversary of the 1910 Revolution**, national holiday, Mexico City: parade and sports exhibitions.
22—**Feria de Santa Cecilia**, San Cristóbal de las Casas, Chiapas.
23-24—**Fiesta de la Caridad**, San Cristóbal de las Casas, Chiapas.

December

8—**Festival of Our Lady of Health**, Pátzcuaro, Mich., Tarascan pilgrimage, dances, fair.
12—**Día de Nuestra Señora de Guadalupe**, patron saint of Mexico, everywhere; Mexico City: pilgrims from all over the country flock to her shrine; dances; also rousingly celebrated in San Cristóbal de las Casas, Chiapas, and Puerto Vallarta, Jalisco.

16-25—**Las Posadas**, Christmas season.
18—**Festival of Our Lady of Solitude**, Oaxaca, Oax., costumes and dances.
23—**Radish Festival**, Oaxaca, Oax., floral and food arrangements, figures carved from radishes.
24—**Christmas Eve (Nochebuena)**, all Mexico, processions at night, singing, family nativity scenes.
25—**Christmas (Navidad)**, national holiday.
31—**Procession of the Holy Sacrament**, Santa Clara del Cobre, Mich., torch and candlelight procession.
31—**New Year's Eve.**